NOTHING TO STEAL

NANCY SHARMAN

Nothing to Steal

The Story of a Southampton
Childhood

KAYE & WARD

First published by
Kaye & Ward Ltd, 21 New Street, London EC2M 4NT
1977

ISBN 0 7182 1175 8

Typeset in Monotype Plantin by
Gloucester Typesetting Co Ltd
Printed in Great Britain by
Biddles of Guildford

THIS BOOK IS
DEDICATED TO THE MEMORY OF
MY WONDERFUL MOTHER

CONTENTS

PUBLISHER'S NOTE

Nancy Sharman lives with her family and works in Southampton. This is the true story of her childhood and growing-up. However, to preserve privacy, the names of all characters with the exception of members of her own family have been changed.

PROLOGUE

I knew there was a clay pit at Bitterne, or so the other children said. They were building new houses on what had once been a lovely wild stretch of rhododendrons and blackberries. The turned-up earth was like sandy grey cheese. I could just see myself making it into dibstones, by baking it in Mum's oven, and then painting them different colours. My imagination ran riot: I would make dogs, cats, ash-trays, little houses and paint them and sell them. What an idea I thought; I got Dorothy and my friend, Audrey, to come with me. We hadn't thought of taking any paper or bags to put the clay in.

After a long walk to the clay pit, we looked around for pieces of wood to prize out the stuff. We found some old tins and discarded newspapers. We filled and wrapped our treasures in them. We had got ourselves pretty mucky by now; Dorothy and Audrey had clay smeared on their faces and clinging to their hair. Homewards we trudged with our tins and newspaper parcels. The coast was clear for Mum was out at work. As I opened the front door with a dirty hand, I left my trade mark of oozy clay on it, which I then wiped off with the hem of my dress.

Through the passage and the living room we went in our clay-encrusted shoes — like the platform soles of today — and into the kitchen, where the red-tiled floor was kept spotless by Mum. There was a good clear space in the middle of the floor; and the three of us, with knives from the kitchen drawer, and Mum's washing-up bowl, worked happily away at moulding our clay. When we had made our shapes, I took Mum's enamel plates, and her big baking dish, and filled these with our creations. We used the water in the bowl, by the way, to smooth the clay after we had made the shapes to our liking. Now for the big moment! To light the gas and bake our clay shapes hard — it seemed all so simple! The floor, our clothes, and everything that we had touched were now dirty and messy. So, while the clay was baking, we set about cleaning up. We worked very hard, but it seemed as if we could never get rid of the damned stuff.

The floor was now a pool of gritty putty; it was easy enough putting the water on it, but we just couldn't seem to mop it up again. We three worked very hard, but now all the fun seemed to have gone out of our efforts; however, we were reasonably satisfied with our cleaning-up operation. Now, we could take the 'objets d'art' out of the oven. They were very hot. We gingerly placed them on newspaper to cool, and set about washing the plates and baking tin. There was more mess now in Mum's sink, so we left the tap running with the plug in to soak the heavily-clayed utensils. As we gazed with rapt attention at our shapes, and wondered if those little cracks in them would get any worse, the sink over-flowed, and we had to set to again to mop up. Our shoes were now wet through, as were our dresses and Mum's kitchen mat by the sink. We opened the door and threw the mat outside into the garden. The mat by the door was also wet, so that went out as well. Turning our attention once more to our clay figures, Dorothy picked up her clay dog by its head; the head remained in her fingers while the body remained on the ground. I gave the dibs a tentative poke; they seemed to be all right. I hurriedly picked up five of them to try them out. I, as quickly, dropped them as they were still hot, and they fell in pieces to the floor. It has been a complete washout in more senses than one. Our disappointment was almost tangible. The door opened, and we heard the tread of Uncle Joe's heavy feet. 'My God, what have you been up to?' he shouted. In a babble of voices, we tried to explain.

I could now see Dorothy and Audrey as they really were; they looked both filthy and wet. I felt strangely dirty, too. The kitchen took on a new appearance as well. I was now very aware that it was filthy. Dorothy tried to show Uncle Joe the cat that she had made. The lump of cat-shaped clay then had the audacity to let its tail fall off. Uncle Joe was as mad as hell. He grabbed me by the arm and dragged me through the living room and passage, pointing out the odd lumps of clay that our shoes had deposited. My friend, Audrey, was sent straight home. I was ordered to wash my hair and Dorothy's, and then to wash all over. 'And make sure you're

clean, my girl,' Uncle threatened, 'for you are both going straight
to bed as a punishment. I'll try to clean up all this mess before
your mother gets in.'

I took a kettle from the hob and did as I was told. I washed our
hair first, then we stood in the bowl on the floor and washed our
feet and legs. I got soap in Dorothy's eyes, and what with Uncle
thundering about and her crying, and me feeling miserable, it was
all most unpleasant. Out of the corner of my eye, I could see Uncle
flinging our clay figures out into the garden and taking the mats
from the front of the house to the back, all the while muttering
under his breath. He didn't hit us, as he was always a gentle kind
man at heart.

We went to bed while Uncle washed the lino in the passage and
living room and cleared up the kitchen, which was then in perfect
condition by the time that Mum got home from work. He even
washed our dresses, and cleaned our shoes, putting them on the
rack over the stove to dry. We had got off very lightly, but we
didn't fancy ourselves as potters ever again. Mum let us come
down for a little while that evening for a cup of cocoa and bread
and marge.

PART ONE

OPEN DOORS

I

My paternal grandmother was an emigré gipsy from Ireland, so I was told, but I never saw her or my grandfather, as they were both dead before I was born. My maternal grandfather was a labourer, who was dead, but my grandmother lived until I was two; I cannot remember her at all. She had eighteen children, thirteen of whom survived – ten boys and three girls. Mum was the second youngest and Uncle Joe the youngest; they were to be close for the rest of their lives. Gran, Mum used to say, was a strict but loving parent and she was renowned for her knowledge of simple remedies, which my Aunt Flo seemed to have inherited. One of this Aunt Flo's grandchildren is alive today, simply because she wouldn't take 'No' for an answer: the doctor had told her that there was no hope for a premature blue scrap of four pounds, but Aunt Flo fed the baby on brandy and water, using an ordinary fountain pen filler, and laid it on cotton wool soaked with olive oil. The baby was not washed for three weeks. She was justifiably proud when the doctor later described her as 'a clever and stubborn woman'.

What I can remember of my father is mostly unpleasant: my most vivid memory being of him taunting my mother as she cowered in a corner of the big bedroom. He was waving a long curved sword about her head and just missed her with each sweep of the sword. I was screaming and tugging at his trouser leg to make him stop. When I was older, I asked Mum, 'Why on earth did you put up with it from him?' She replied that he was her man and that she could not help herself. 'You just can't stop loving someone, like turning off a tap,' Mum said.

I was born in 1925, the second of three children by Mum's first marriage. My brother Ken was two years older than me and my sister Dorothy two years younger. My father was, in all probability, an alcoholic but in those days alcoholism was little understood. He frequently arrived home in such a state that he would fall to the floor dead drunk. He was too heavy for Mum to lift, so she just covered him with a coat; he often stayed on the floor all night. His drunken temper was horrible. My brother Ken was thrashed with a belt for coming in late from school or swinging on the gate; in addition, he was sent to bed without supper for the last offence. Mum sneaked upstairs with some bread for him, but was caught in the act, and got a hiding from my father. How Ken managed to keep his lovely sunny disposition despite those early years I find very hard to understand.

My father was both extremely handsome and very domineering. Mum said that the men who worked for him were afraid of him; certainly Mum and her three children were. Try as hard as I may, I cannot remember anything good about him, not a single kind trait. His mania for weapons, which covered most walls in the house, was a perpetual reminder of his violence: there were swords, pistols, guns, scimitars, daggers, spears, helmets, shields, gauntlets, and halberds! Although he had treated her badly from the beginning, Mum loved him and kept coming back for more. Fortunately for her, she had a wonderful mother and sisters who always seemed to be taking us into their homes. Children are very resilient, so Ken, Dorothy and myself can look back on a happy childhood. Mum, I used to think, was the most beautiful woman in the world: her hair was thick and wavy and rather dark. Curly tendrils caressed her temples and the nape of her neck. She wore her hair in a bun and used the same large pins for years on end. We children loved to see her let her hair down at night, when it covered her shoulders like a cape. Her eyes were dark, like a doe's, and her nose and mouth were pleasantly formed; she never needed make-up. Of medium height, she had a lovely figure which looked neat from any angle. Her voice was soft, and she was full of love for her children. She seemed incapable of having bad thoughts about people, for she could always see the other person's point-of-view. She looked for the best in everyone, and I used to think that she could have found an excuse for the devil himself. 'Everyone has some good in them,' Mum would say. Apart from her supreme gentleness, she had more guts than anybody else that I ever knew, and her fortitude in adversity was magnificent. Mum was really too soft for the

Mum at nineteen years old

harsh treatment which she received from life, but she rarely grumbled about it; 'You can always see somebody else worse off', she would say.

The only time Mum ever stopped working was when she took to bed for child-birth or was desperately ill. Poor Mum just did not have any luck with men: none that she had were any good and she really deserved the best.

My father's name was Frank, but he was always called Stiffy – short for 'Big Stiff'. He was six foot four inches in his socks, and built like Hercules with curly brown hair and bold brown eyes. I did not like his eyes; they seemed to bore into one. He was a boss stevedore in Southampton Docks. That is to say he negotiated with individual owners and captains of ships for the loading and unloading of cargoes. Unemployment was so bad then that men would literally fawn upon him, in the hope of being taken on for work. Some would buy him drinks which they could ill afford. I can remember seeing men standing, cap in hand, while he paid them at the kitchen table, on which stood little piles of silver in neat rows. As each man received his due, he would say 'Thanks Stiffy, see you later.' No doubt he drank some of their wages. He boasted of drinking eighteen pints a night, plus shorts. My father had a dominating, sadistic personality: he not only domineered in a mental sense but used his great strength to overpower whoever he decided he would like to torment.

He was always laughing, or so it seemed, when he was not in a rage. One had to be wary of Dad's laughter. It was not *with* people that he laughed, it was *at* their discomfort. He seemed to have the very devil inside him.

My Uncle Jack, his brother, was a much smaller man, and a cripple, with a club-foot. My father met Uncle Jack and his girl in Britannia Road. They were walking towards each other. Dad decided that they should go with him in the opposite direction to a pub. In vain they protested as the girl did not drink at all, coming from a teetotal family. After a semi-jocular argument, with Dad's temper rising, he just picked up the slight form of the girl, put her over his shoulder and strolled off towards the pub. Uncle Jack followed, limping along and powerless to prevent my father. The young couple had to lump it and Uncle Jack's girl ended up drinking a lemonade in a pub. She slipped away with Uncle as soon as they could and, although she later became Dad's sister-in-law, she never forgave him.

Dad's sadism took many forms. He thought it funny to manacle my brother Ken by tying his ankles loosely together so that he could just about shuffle along. Ken would then be pricked with a long sword to make him move. Dad would roar with laughter at the antics of the small boy trying to get away from the sharp point of the sword. Mum would protest helplessly. 'It's only a joke, woman,' Dad would say. 'He'll suffer worse at school. Let's make a man of him.' Ken suffered most at the hands of my father: it was usually a good belting he got. Dorothy, my younger sister, was his favourite and would laugh at his games which delighted him. He would fill her pants with knives and forks, throw her up and catch her. Dorothy's shrill screams of delight satisfied some wildness in him. He would take her on the big dipper at the fair, or on the chair-planes, when she was barely two, and she loved it. Dad had plenty of money. He would take his darling Dorothy into a shop, tell the assistant that he wanted a complete new set of clothes for her and, choosing only what he liked, would buy a complete wardrobe of clothes. The clothes that Dorothy wore on entering the shop would be disdainfully left behind.

We had a large Alsatian dog, Pat, who was an ex-German police dog. Dad bought him from a captain of a boat from Hamburg. Pat was believed to be untrainable, for his previous owners could not cope with him. To my father, Pat was a challenge, and the dog soon realized who was boss. Pat was all right with Ken and Dorothy; Mum he just about tolerated, but he terrified me. I knew that he knew I was frightened of him. When Dad took Pat out on a lead the pavements would clear as if by magic. Neighbours who knew of Pat's temperament promptly vanished at his approach. One day, a man from a few doors up, whom my father did not like, rebuked him for the way he handled the Alsatian. My father smiled at the man but his eyes should have warned the interfering neighbour. 'Perhaps you think that you would look after him better,' Dad suggested. 'I would,' came the reply. 'In that case, you can have him! Let me wrap the lead around your wrist several times, he is a strong one and pulls mighty hard. All right Pat, off you go my lad, off you go with your new owner!' The new owner coaxed Pat in a pleasant voice, 'Come along Patty, off we go.' Pat looked uncertainly at the two men then, at a sharp command from my father, Pat moved off, looking round with a worried expression at my father every few steps. So they proceeded some 30 yards up the road. Putting his fingers in his mouth, Dad then whistled Pat who dragged his 'owner', with the lead wrapped firmly round his hand and wrist, back to suffer further torment. 'Guard him Pat', said Dad. The Alsatian stood over the prostrate man, fangs showing and making a low throaty growl. The victim could not move for fear. 'Why don't you tell your dog to go away,' laughed Dad. 'I can see that he's very fond of you; he looks as if he'd like to eat you. How long do you think you will be down there playing with him . . . ?' Dad enjoyed himself no end and kept the teasing up until it ceased to amuse him. He told his neighbour not to interfere again, or he would not get off so lightly. The wretched man shakily made his way back to his house on trembling legs.

Dad had a great deal of money. His wallet always bulged with notes and his pockets were heavy with silver. Mum did not get much of it, for he was downright mean over the housekeeping money. As long as he had what he wanted to eat, he wasn't in the least concerned with what she had. She had to give him the best of everything. He came in very late and well boozed one Saturday afternoon long after the pubs had closed. Dad looked at his dinner, which Mum had placed on the table as soon as he entered the room. The food was rather dry, even though Mum had done her best to keep it hot. Dad well knew that it was a better meal than Mum had eaten. He said that it was hardly fit for a dog and put it on the floor. Mum had to watch Pat gulp the food which she herself would have enjoyed eating. Dad then went upstairs to sleep off the drink.

One evening, Dad sent Mum out with Ken and me, to get some faggots and peas for his supper. There was a 'faggot & peas shop' some fifteen minutes away, if one hurried. Northam people took their own basins or dishes to be filled with cooked dried peas and lovely savoury balls of faggots; and, of course, something to cover the food and keep it warm. The shop would sell only these two commodities, and was open at dinner times and in the evenings. Dorothy was left at home with Dad. I suppose, allowing time for going to the place, waiting to be served, and hurrying home, we had been gone about thirty minutes. Mum had to knock on the door when we returned because Dad had locked it. When Dad opened the door, he complained that he had been kept waiting too long, took the basin from Mum, then shut the door in our faces. We hung about for a while, with Mum giving the door an occasional knock. It was getting cold and Mum was becoming concerned about Dorothy.

We went to Aunty's house which was three streets away to get help. Mum wondered if anybody would be willing to force open the front window for her. A neighbour, by name Mr Fenchurch, said that he would oblige. We all returned to the house. Mr Fenchurch set to work on the front window and in no time at all we were in the house. Mum thanked the kind neighbour and he departed. She then closed the window and we made our way, gingerly, to the living room. Dad was enjoying himself if his laughter was anything to go by; we could hear Dorothy laughing too. When Mum opened the door, we saw a strange sight: Dad had thrown all the floor mats into the kitchen and was playing billiards on the lino with some of the faggots and a walking stick! He seemed in quite a good mood and appeared not to find it strange that we should have returned home by way of the front window.

Because of Dad's outrageous behaviour, the next door neighbour was always looking in at the living room window, or so Dad thought. The houses were terraced, and the windows of our and their living room were some eight feet apart. So as to discourage the woman next door from spying on him, Dad wrote ARSEHOLES, in large, whitewashed letters, on our window. A furious neighbour came to remonstrate with him. 'If the nosey cow didn't want to read it . . .', she was told, 'don't look.' This neighbour was a plucky woman and insisted upon Dad cleaning the letters off. He became quite charming and the woman was mollified. He had invited her into the house and she was able to watch him wipe it off. So, with a satisfied smile, she left. Before she had got indoors, Dad had replaced the offending word with something worse, REPEAT, REPEAT, REPEAT. Our neighbour couldn't win. She felt sorry for Mum, having some idea of what Mum had to put up with, and things remained as they were.

We three children lived with Mum and Dad in Radcliffe Road but it was a sort of 'off and on' existence. On one occasion when Mum left him, taking us with her to Gran's, Dad was determined to take Dorothy back from her. He found his opportunity when we were all together on a tram: he jumped on the moving tram, grabbed Dorothy from Mum's arms, and jumped off. Mum left him, or was thrown out so many times, that it became a little confusing for me, not being at all sure where I lived.

I can distinctly remember the eleven different places I had lived in and the six different schools I had attended before I was seven and Dad died. Our home, if it could be called that, was moved on a handcart, at sixpence an hour, being pushed by some sympathetic relation, with us kids trailing along behind. How I remember it! The house was full of little treasures which he had always collected. Clocks, pictures, brass-work, silver antiques, a magnificent four-poster bed with brick red hangings. Dad also owned a small yacht, the boat left at a wharf while the sails and mast were kept along the passage, from where they reached to the top of the stairs. He had them brought to the house because he was not well enough to sail. Dad also had a little red sports car, which was really something for that area of Southampton.

Mum told me when I was older that the first time Dad had brought Ivy, his mistress, to our home, the three of them had spent an awkward evening sitting round the living-room table. Dad had been adamant about Ivy staying. Mum went up to bed determined to stick it out, for this time Dad had surely gone too far? She thought he would have to give in and send Ivy packing. She lay in the bed, listening for the sounds of Ivy's departure. Then she heard two sets of footsteps on the stairs. Dad and Ivy entered the bedroom; Dad undressed, pushed Mum over to the other side of the bed and got into the middle, then he pulled the other, still fully-clothed, female in beside him. In the small hours a thoroughly miserable Mum gathered up her children and our clothes and left him. Mum always hated green things because of Ivy. For the rest of her life, she chose any other colour but green for the home or clothes.

When he first became ill, the Doctor told him to stop drinking and to eat well if he was to have any chance of recovery. He tried this for a while but his need for alcohol had become too great. He even tried a gipsy remedy, which required taking snails from their shells and, after pricking their slug-like bodies, drinking the liquid so obtained. He concluded that if he was going to die, then he would go out with a bang; he had nothing to lose. So, from then on he drank all he wanted, dragging his unwilling body to clubs, pubs and parties with the aid of two walking sticks. He finished himself off within five months.

Mum was beside herself with grief. She had no pride where her love for him was concerned. She had been going in to see him every night. Towards the end it must have been hell, having her own front door opened for her by Ivy, the other woman. She had to go out to work during the day to keep herself and us children. We were then living at her sister's house. It was decided that we would return to the house after the funeral; in that way she thought that it would be like going back for a fresh start. The house automatically became Mum's on his death, as Dad had been buying it when he became ill. There was also a little insurance money for her. I didn't feel much when Mum told us that our Daddy was dead as we had not been living with him for some time. Ken, however, simply said, 'I'm glad, good riddance!' He was just nine years old.

For Ken and me, all Dad had left was a roof over our heads and some unpleasant memories. I can remember the envelopes with the black edges which were to be sent to invited mourners and the glass domed cases of wax flowers which arrived at Aunty's house. For the funeral, Mum, Ken, Dorothy and I were all dressed in new clothes. Mum had a veil over her face and was completely swathed in black. We walked from Aunty's to our old home, but we did not go inside. Instead we entered the funeral carriages waiting outside. I thought it was nice to ride in such a splendid carriage and I was especially pleased with my new shoes – they were shiny black with a silver buckle. I felt quite important sitting up there in my new clothes: it was indeed a charming novelty for me. I can also remember the scene at the graveside very clearly. I was most impressed by the large number of those glass domed wax flowers. Mum's comment was that all the pubs which Dad had frequented must have sent one.

More than anything else, Ken and I were looking forward to going back to our old house without Dad being there. When the funeral was over, a car collected a weeping Mum, my Aunt and us three children outside the cemetery gates and we all returned to Radcliffe Road. This was the first time that Mum had set foot in it for about a week. It was now practically bare. There was a table and four chairs in the living room plus a few other odd bits-and-pieces of worthless furniture downstairs; and a couple of beds, with a chest of drawers and a dressing table, upstairs. The only worthwhile item of furniture left was a chiffonier in the front room; this was so big that it took up all one side of the room and would have had to have been dismantled in order to get it out of the house. It was too much for whoever had taken the rest of the furniture, although somebody must have struggled out with the mast and the sails as they were gone. Mum thought it must have been a two-man job. However, nobody ever owned-up to taking any of the furniture and Mum was so miserable at Dad's death that she didn't care. She was just disgusted that people could do such things and gave a tired little laugh, saying 'I suppose I should be grateful that they left the lino on the floor and the kitchen sink.' Pat, the Alsatian, had been put down so we really had the house to ourselves.

Mum told me that even Dad's departure from the surface of this planet had a touch of the flamboyant and bizarre. Four unrelated females were seen when the coffin was lowered into the trench, standing at the back of the group at the graveside. They all had one thing in common for, apart from Ivy, each of the other three had been, at one time or another, a mistress of my father. Such charisma did Dad's spirit extend that they had felt compelled to attend his funeral.

II

One of the first jobs Ken was given was to pull the pretty ivy off the garden wall and burn it in the incinerator. Mum felt better with that reminder gone. It didn't take long to collect our clothes from Aunty's. With the insurance money, Mum took us to Bournemouth for the day and we even had a snap taken on the beach. We were making a fresh start. It was going to be a struggle for Mum, but she was determined to try to keep her little band together. She was now to be the breadwinnner for us, and bread was to be the word! The only money that Mum earned came from back-breaking, cleaning jobs. Her poor hands were a terrible sight, with chaps like knife-cuts on her fingers and knuckles from the soda in the water she used for scrubbing. She did not have a widow's pension as my father had never paid any insurance stamps.

Sometimes I used to stay with Aunt Bell, who was so fat and round and cuddly and always full of high spirits. She had dark hair and there was a little fuzzy moustache always to be seen on her upper lip. She must have had a great sense of propriety, for after she had bathed me in the big tin bath in front of the fire, she would add more hot for herself and get in with her vest and bloomers on. She had only the one room, so it was difficult to obtain privacy. I loved sleeping in her bed, with its lush feather mattress and very high brass rails at each end. The knobs on the corners unscrewed, and that was where she used to hide the money she didn't want Uncle to know about. She used to chat to me in a conspiratorial manner, as though there was some big secret between us, and once gave me tuppence out of Uncle's trousers, hanging on the rail at the foot of the bed. She winked at me: 'The silly old fool will never miss the money, he was plastered when he came home last night.' The rails of the bed served as a sort of wardrobe, so that it was impossible to see through them.

One night, she had a glass of water into which she put a spoonful of stuff that looked like crushed soda. On the tin was written *Kruschens Salts*. I asked her what it was for, and could I have some, please. 'No, it's not for little girls,' she smilingly said. 'This stuff is for Uncle, and it makes him leap out of bed in the morning, and he can jump right over the end of the bed.' This information was received with astonishment for, if it could do that for big Uncle, I reasoned, just imagine what it could do for a small one like me. If I took two spoonfuls, I would be able to jump twice as high and I might even touch the ceiling. As I lay in bed that night, I determined to get some of the magical potion. I could just see myself springing clear over the end of the rails at the foot of the bed. When Auntie went to the back, I leapt out of bed, and stood on a chair in order to reach the mantelpiece on which the tin was placed. I got a spoon and prised off the lid, just as I had seen Auntie do. I hadn't time to get a glass of water, so I forced two spoonfuls of the horrid stuff down, replaced the tin and hopped back into bed, hardly able to wait for the morning. Instead I spent most of the night on Aunty's big Po. It was far removed from flying up to the ceiling! Mum was told by Aunty that it was her fault, 'I never dreamt that she would take me so literally'. It didn't put me off of staying with Aunty though and she even bought a small enamel pot for future use, as her big white china one with the red roses on the side was really too large for little bottoms.

Another aunt, Maud, had a cat, a canary, a sewing machine and a bicycle, which were all kept in her room at night. All her cooking was done on the open fire, and she had a glorious biscuit tin full of buttons, buckles, ribbons, wools, and even Uncle's Great War medals, which I was allowed to poke around in. She produced crayons and paper at the drop of a hat. The cat sat at the table as if he were one of the family and was always called Mr Tom. The canary was allowed out, when the cat was not around, and Maud would put a piece of apple between her teeth for the bird to peck at. She kept a bubble pipe for children, who could use Uncle's shaving mug for the soapy water. No princess in a castle was ever happier than I was, in that cluttered little room of Aunt Maud's.

I always played very hard at whatever I was doing. For instance, when I played hairdressers, I was the barber and the other children were my customers. The barber's shop was a chair in Aunty Flo's back garden. I took her towel to put round their necks and scissors from my own needlework box, which I had been given for Christmas. My 'customers' were three second cousins and my sister Dorothy. I started on the two smallest boys and cut their hair off to the scalp. My third customer was a girl with long ringlets. I was working away on her, and had only finished one side, when there was an anguished cry from her mother. 'You little devil,' she spat at me, 'I thought you were all too quiet out here!' She snatched the scissors from my hand and gave me a walloping. 'Oh, my God,' she cried, 'Look what you've done to them!' She walloped me again and again, and again. I couldn't understand why she was so angry: we were having a lovely game, I thought.

Some days later, I found my needlework box, which had mysteriously disappeared. It was on a shelf by the side of the fireplace. I took it down and when I opened it, it was full of certificates and Insurance Policies. I could read at quite an early age, for I started school at three. I was probably about four at this time. As I was most put out by the taking of my box, I emptied its contents on to the top of the shelf and took my box away. I wondered where the pretty coloured cottons and the thimble were. I knew who had the scissors. When Aunty Flo found out, she took the box away from me again, and I got another smacking for touching her valuable papers. I didn't think Aunty liked me very much.

The house was really open house for everyone. It always seemed to be full of neighbours and children and was quite chaotic inside. Dogs had puppies in corners and cats had kittens in cupboards. The walls of the passage were strung with washing and the walls of the living room covered by pencilled writing, giving such information as: '2.30 at Doncaster 2d each way,' or, 'the 4 o'clock at Epsom 3d on the nose'. The wall nearest the door was plastered with such graffiti.

The piano in the front room always seemed to have someone banging out a tune and the fireplace always glowed with a cosy red fire. I remembered Aunty Flo peering from behind the curtain and hoping to dodge the Tally man when he came. She said to her small grandson, 'When the man knocks at the door, tell him that Nanny is not in.' When the Tallyman did knock at the door the child reported to him that 'Nanny was not in' and, turning round and looking into the room, the child asked: 'Are you, Nanny?' In this same house, when I was a little older, there was a man's bicycle leaning up against the wall in the passage. It was one of the rare occasions when the house was empty. I had seen boys ride a man's bike by putting one of their legs through the bars and riding it in a sort of sidesaddle fashion. So I thought that I would have a go. The seat was all up in the air and the bicycle seemed very big. I got it out on to the pavement, and on to the street after a struggle. I put my right leg through the bars and tried my luck. I found to my relief that I could manage it. I rode up the street to Britannia Road. Such a lovely long road. And away I went. As I approached the end of the road, I realized that I could not stop and that there was a large brick wall ahead. I shut my eyes and then, BANG! I was on the ground but was not hurt, except for a graze on my forehead. I picked up the bike, which seemed very heavy, and looked at the front wheel, which definitely looked a bit bent. It took me a lot longer to walk back with the bike than it had taken me to ride it down. I carefully put it back in the passage. Later that evening there was a big row about who had done the damage. I thought Aunty Flo gave me a funny look but it was probably only my guilty conscience. I couldn't keep my secret for long and later confessed. Poor Aunty, I'm afraid I was a bit of a trial for her.

I would think that it was before I was seven, that I was 'left' with a lady whom Mum called Bet. 'I'll pick her up tomorrow, Bet. Thank you for having her,' she said and, turning to me, continued, 'Be a good girl, now', and with a kiss on the cheek, was gone. I went with Bet into her house where she gave me a jigsaw puzzle to keep me occupied and a piece of cake to eat. She sat me at a little table in a corner behind the door and I was soon engrossed in my jigsaw. I looked up, however, when the door was opened and a jolly, smiling man entered. On a large dinner plate held low down in front of him was a messy, hairy, mauvy-brownish thing. 'Here you are, Bet,' he said. 'Here's some good red meat for your dinner.' He caught sight of me and was horrified at seeing a child in the room. He quickly disappeared, with his plate of genitals.

I didn't see much more of him that day and when evening came, I was put to sleep in a big feather mattressed bed, in a strange dark room. I was frightened. I heard a mouse gnawing away in a corner. I thought it was in a cupboard, and I put my head under the bed-clothes hoping not to hear it, but it didn't make any difference. Much later Bet and the jolly man came to bed — my bed! The springs began moving and making a noise, and so did Bet. I pre-tended to fidget in my sleep to make him stop because I thought that he was hurting her. 'Ssshh!' whispered Bet. 'You'll wake the kid.' They got out of bed and finished their business against the wall.

III

At the top of our road was an entrance to a coal depot and on the wall outside was a notice with large white capital letters – BILL STICKERS WILL BE PROSECUTED. I knew a boy by the name of Bill and wondered what this other Bill Stickers had done to be wanted by the police. He must have been on the run a long time, I thought, because the notice had been there for as long as I could remember. When I was passing by there with Ken one day, I asked 'Why are they persecuting Bill Stickers? What has he done?' 'You daft thing', he replied. 'The word is prosecuted, not persecuted' (I was always getting my words mixed up) 'and it means a man that sticks bills on the wall. Bill Stickers is not a man's name. You are silly, our Nance!'

This boy I knew, called Bill, was a nasty, cruel lad of some eight years of age, I think. I know he was older than me. He used to stick pins into living insects and pull off their legs and wings; he cut worms in half with his rusty knife, as well. Alice, a much older girl who lived next door to Bill, told me that he buried a spider alive in a matchbox, and after covering it with dirt, he made a cross out of matchsticks tied with cotton and then said a prayer over it. Alice had seen him tormenting insects from over her garden wall. She also naturally disliked him because he had hit her small brother. Alice 'had it in' for Bill. I was only one of the small fry who happened to be there when she took her revenge. Some workmen had dug a deep hole in the pavement near her house and left the gravel piled high around the sides. They had gone off to have their dinner and their picks and shovels were leaning up against the wall. If you were on the house side you wouldn't realize that there was a deep hole on the other side of the gravel. As Bill came out of his gate, Alice provocatively said, 'I bet you couldn't jump over that heap, Bill.' 'I bet I could,' Bill retorted. 'Go on then, let's see you, big mouth,' Alice gibed. The silly lad ran up to the gravel, leapt high in the air, and failing to land on the non-existent pavement, vanished down the hole, with screams. We all rushed to look at the damage; Bill didn't look very well. 'Don't they give people who faint a drink of water?' Alice said sarcastically. 'Wait a minute, I'll get him some.' She flew indoors and came out with an old rusty tin can. 'It's fresh out of the lavatory,' she called down to the recumbent Bill and poured it over him. 'Now perhaps you'll leave our nipper alone, you rotten thing, you!' Alice crowed. I must admit that I too enjoyed Bill's discomfort. As he climbed out of the hole, looking much the worse for wear, Alice put her foot out and tripped him up. We all tittered and laughed as the door closed behind Bill. He never bothered Alice's nipper again.

There was a terrible boy in one house at which I stayed. He was always pinching me and pulling the elastic on my knickers. When I bent over to get something from a cupboard, he caressed my bottom, and he was always saying: 'Let me show you my thing, it's got real hairs coming on it'. Other favourite sayings of his were: 'That's our bread you're eating; that's my Mum's soap you're using; my Mum got those shoes for you; my Mum is ever so good to take you in'. He was the most hateful boy that I ever met. One day, as his Mum was going out, I said to her 'Can I come with you?' 'No,' she replied. 'You stay in and play with Billy'. 'Oh, *please* let me come with you,' I implored her. 'No, you can't,' she said. 'And stop making such a fuss!' I made more fuss and started to cry. 'Come on now, love,' she coaxed, 'What's it all about?' I told her about horrible Billy. Her manner completely changed. 'You are a nasty little girl. My Billy wouldn't behave like that; you are making up stories. Policemen take naughty girls away!' She knew, however, that I wasn't making up stories, for Billy *was* just like his Dad – a chip off the old block. I had seen his Dad pat the bottom of any female who entered the house: it didn't matter if they were 7 or 70 – he couldn't keep his hands off their backsides. Some of his victims brushed his hand aside and looked annoyed, while others took it all in good part. He didn't dare, however, to do it while his wife was around. His Mum must have said something to my tormentor, because he looked daggers at me. The next day I was taken to another Aunty.

At a quarter-to-nine the bell over the Infants' section of Northam School would start to peal, 'Ding, Dong, Come to School, Ding, Dong, Come to School'. The caretaker who rang it was never late, and as the bell could be heard clearly all over Northam, we had no excuse for not being on time. On the way to school, we always stopped by Martins the bakers, on the corner of Northam Road and Kent Street, for such mouth-watering smells here filled the air. Along the side of the shop, just above pavement level, were some small dusty windows, and we could look down and see the bakers at work. Two or three of them were to be seen in their tall white hats, with well-floured arms handling trays of bread or cakes ready for baking. When they plonked a small round lump of dough on a bigger lump, I knew that was to be a cottage loaf. Occasionally, we were lucky enough to see the dough plaited. Each loaf was quite individual in shape and yet how they could grab a handful of dough to make each loaf near enough the same was always a mystery to me. The windows at the front of Martins were crammed with fancy cakes, pies and doughnuts. For me they were only to look at, since Mum never bought anything there.

We bought our bread at the back of Price's bakery – a yesterday's loaf, which was cheaper. Bread was 2½d large, and 1¾d small, at full price. The only problem about going to the back of Price's was the horses. We had to wait until they had finished their rounds for the day, for what was left over was considered stale and not fit for tomorrow's delivery, though prized by us. The horses and carts were lined up on each side of the yard, some twelve in all, and I was fearful of walking through the middle of them. The horses didn't look very good-tempered to me. I needed all my courage to pass through but if I could get a friend, or my sister Dorothy, to accompany me then it wasn't so bad. I noticed, however, that even

This was Mum's corner shop when I was a child

my friends who weren't afraid of horses, nipped smartly out the way if a huge head turned towards us. They generally had their heads tucked down in their feeding bags and I was always grateful to get away unscathed with my loaf. It was no good telling grown-ups that you were scared. It was all right for them, they were all up there, and I was all down here: my head was about as high as the belly of the great beast. When they swung their heads round and I stared straight up into their nostrils, they looked as fierce as dragons to me.

I often had to wear second-hand shoes, some of which were not only ugly in appearance, but too tight in fit. When I grumbled to Mum about one such pair, she trotted out another of her 'wise' sayings: 'I cried because I had no shoes, until I met a man who had no feet'. What could a child answer to that? There was no answer. It seemed that Mum had a proverb to match any situation. If we did not have much to eat, she would say, 'Half a loaf is better than no bread at all'. Once I hurt my own feet deliberately. I was playing in the front with Sadie, Dorothy and some other girls, when down the road came Nora. Nora was everything that I was not. She was dainty, pretty and rich – for both her parents were working. She was also a spoilt brat, who owned tap-dancing shoes and ballet shoes. 'You ought to let me be in your show,' she said. 'I can do anything, and my dancing teacher said that I might be famous when I grow up. My Mummy says that I'm sure to go on the stage'. That did it. 'Just because you have dancing shoes, that doesn't mean that you can dance,' I jeered. 'I can dance better than you anyway,' Nora crowed. 'Go on then,' I gibed, 'go and get your dance shoes and we'll see'. I had been thinking of shoes for tap-dancing, not ballet shoes. I wasn't much good at ballet.

Nora ran to her house and was back in a flash wearing her pumps. She started to perform at once. She was a very pretty sight, twinkling away with grace and ease on that gritty pavement. I had opened my big mouth, so I had to have a go. I got up in my already uncomfortable second-hand shoes and began to dance. It was agony but I persevered. I tottered about like a constipated kangaroo, doing my best to keep my end up. I concluded with the dying swan bit, as gracefully as I could, but I think I must have looked to the onlookers more like a plucked chicken. My friends nevertheless, applauded loudly. 'That's not ballet!' expostulated Nora. 'Nance was better than you,' cried the loyal Sadie. 'You lost,

so beat it Nora, we don't want you!' It was a hollow victory: both
Nora and I knew who the best dancer was, but poor Nora never
fitted in down our road.

There always seemed to be something for Northam children to
do – never a dull moment, you might say. Cattle, as many as fifty
or sixty at one time, were driven from outlying country districts
through the streets to the Cattle Market at the lower end of
Southampton. I thought he was a very brave man who ordered the
large beasts about, though armed with only a wooden staff. We
children would follow behind, at a safe distance, as we were a little
awed by the creatures. It was enough to make us die of fright, when
a great horned head swung round and one was faced by a wet nose
and mouth, and those large brown eyes with the long lashes. If the
cow actually went 'MOO' shivers of excitement would run through
us.

The sheep that we also followed were not quite so frightening.
They used to be allowed to rest in the graveyard of St Mary's
church and would placidly graze among the tombstones. I tried to
work out the pattern of life: the sheep ate the grass; the grass was
rich because of the soil being fed by all those decomposing bodies;
then people ate the sheep. In my young and fanciful way, I thought
it was almost like being a cannibal. We would follow the sheep to
the market and stand watching all the doomed sheep and chickens.
I used to wonder if they felt sad, knowing they were going to die.
I now realize that cows often have wet, tearful looking eyes, but in
those childhood days, I suspected that they were crying.

St Mary's church had wonderful bells, and on quiet Sunday
mornings or evenings they would peal out their glorious sounds.
The song 'The Bells of St Mary's' is supposed to have been
inspired by those in Southampton.

We usually went to the Floating Bridge when the market closed.
We hoped to be in time for a bit of fun. What we children thought
was fun was a good wetting for others. Once in a blue moon, some
fool would rush down the gravel slope on his bike in an attempt to
catch the Floating Bridge as it pulled out. We much appreciated
the free show when the bike didn't make it, and rider and frame
ended up in the water. An old Ford car tried it on one occasion,
where the foreshore shelved steeply because the tide was going out.
We watched with baited breath as the Ford just missed the bridge
and plunged in, with the river water coming up to its windows. It

had made our extra journey worthwhile, and we cheered as the dripping man was helped from his water-logged car. It was a $\frac{1}{2}$d fare on the floating bridge for under-fourteens and whole gangs of children would ride to and fro looking through the little windows at the great, brass-festooned engines which drove the ferry. Eventually, the man-in-charge, his patience exhausted, would chase us off and at last we would go home.

On the Woolston side of the Floating Bridge were the Super-Marine works. The Schneider Trophy planes were built there and my Uncle Joe would never fail to tell me how clever the British were. He was very proud of being British and you might have thought that he had helped to build the planes, he waxed so lyrical about them. Super-Marine was to be the birthplace of the Spitfire.

Chapel district, where the market was, was divided from Woolston by the river Itchen. Uncle used to joke that when people crossed on the ferry, they 'came over Itchen and went back Scratchin'. All along the river Itchen were small wharves where people from adjoining districts would come to watch their own regatta. The Coalporters Rowing Club was well supported when they rowed against other teams. They were a Northam-based club, having their headquarters at the back of the Yacht Tavern at the end of Britannia Road. We Northamites would line our bit of shore and cheer our local heroes with wild enthusiasm at regatta times.

We children used to go to church or Sunday School three times on a Sunday: morning, afternoon and evening. It didn't matter what the denomination of the church was, for it all had little to do with religion. We had to go, for it got us out of the house, and let the grown-ups snatch some peace. Attendance at church just before Christmas was most important, in any case. We didn't want any absentee marks on our cards, because tha. might mean missing the Christmas party. An occasion not to be missed, indeed, for not only would there be a second-hand present, but jelly and custard and cakes as well. I always took a paper bag and made sure that I got something to put in it if any cakes were left over. Several other greedy hands would be doing the same!

One party I always remember because there was a Christmas tree with a little red handbag at the very top. I wanted that bag so much. As the presents came off one by one, until there were only a

The floating bridge, showing the shore on either side:
Woolston and townside

few children left, the bag seemed certain to be mine. I was one of
the very last because I was tall and looked older than my years.
Then the little red bag went to the girl in front of me and I was
given a jigsaw puzzle instead. On the way home, I was so disappointed that I threw the jigsaw over a wall. When Mum asked
me where my present was, Dorothy chimed in, 'She threw it over
the wall, Mum, she could have given it to me.' 'You are a wicked
girl,' Mum said. 'You don't deserve to go to parties. Beggars can't
be choosers'. Many years later I bought my own small daughter a
red handbag; it gave me much satisfaction.

IV

I couldn't stand it when Mum was cross with me. It seemed then
as though a big black cloud hung over me. When I was sent to bed
early one night as a punishment for being naughty, I thought to

myself, 'I'll climb out of the window and run away, then she'll be sorry that she made me cry'. I could see her in my mind's eye, wringing her hands and looking for her runaway daughter, and being sad because she wouldn't see me again. I didn't see her next morning as she had gone to work, and rather than go home after school at tea-time, I hung about the streets until it was dark, when my stomach drove me in. Mum had gone back to work by then, so she knew nothing of my silly thoughts: all that hanging about and going without my tea for nothing. When I told her, she replied, 'Never cut off your nose to spite your face. Silly girl, of course I love you, but Mummy gets tired sometimes and she hasn't got as much patience as she should have'.

My sister Dorothy was such a pretty little girl, with dark bobbed hair, bright brown eyes and round face. Also, as she was often ill, she was the centre of attention. I loved her dearly but she had a terrible temper and liked having her own way. I remember once having a bath, when we were at Aunt Bell's, but Dorothy didn't want to follow me. It took Uncle, Mum and Aunty to hold her down in the water and they were all soaked by the time that they had finished with Dorothy – and she was only four years old! When it came to birthdays (mine was the 16th of June and Dorothy's on the 26th) she made such a fuss that Mum had to give her a present on my birthday as well, yet for me there was just the one present. I didn't mind at all, I was such a placid child. Not much to look at either. When someone had to run an errand, Ken would say, 'I'm not going, make one of them go'. Dorothy would say, 'I'm not going, make our Nance go', and, whack across the bottom, our Nance would go. When I complained to Mum about it later, she said, 'You were always the most willing of the three, that's why you got moved around so much.'

There wasn't much space in our living room but we girls had one drawer each for our treasures. Ken had the bottom of a sideboard. He was a nice-looking boy, with brown hair and brown eyes, and I was very proud of him – he was so clever. He was always making things with his knife – boats and planes and catapults. His cupboard seemed like Aladdin's cave to me: there were comics and marbles, books and string cords, conkers, dead bats, everything that boys find essential for living. Ken had a Meccano set which I thought was the 'cat's-whiskers'. He treated us lesser mortals with haughty contempt, and he warned me severely about going to his

cupboard again: 'If you go there again, I'll know about it!' I did
not take his advice. I waited with Dorothy until he had gone out
and then we opened the door of Aladdin's cave. Right at the back
there was a torch and, as I put my hand in to get it, I dislodged lots
of tiny ball bearings. The cheeky blighter had rigged his cupboard.
I had broken a piece of black cotton when feeling with my hand
which then let loose the ball bearings. No wonder that he had said
that he would 'know about it'. I felt more pride in his ingenuity
than fear at being found out. We all used to get on very well, in
fact, and there were few real quarrels. I only tried to fight Ken
when he teased me and he would just stick out his long arm so that
I couldn't get near enough to punch him: he only laughed at me.
If ever I required protection, loyal Ken was always the first to my
defence.

When the Fair was coming to the Common, we would do our
best to acquire some pennies. We visited our Uncles and Aunties
in the hope that they would part with a few coppers and also
bummed rags and jam-jars to sell to the rag man. The rag man's
shop always had a foul stink, for he had piles of meat bones and we
would disturb a cloud of metallic green flies, which would return
heavily to their stinking meal when we had passed. In a gang, we
children, together with our hard-gained pennies, would spend the
rest of the day at the fair. We did more looking about than anything else. We never actually saw the Fat Lady or the Bearded
Lady or the calf with five legs. Just to stand outside the colourful
tents and listen to the fairground barkers inviting customers in 'for
only 3d' to see 'The Wonderful show', 'The only one in the world'
and 'You'll be amazed', was excitement enough. We would tramp
from one end of the fair to the other, not missing a stall or a show.
One of the bigger boys with us, Jack, tried to squeeze under a tent
to see the boxing and got his trousers half pulled off by the man
who dragged him out. At another stall, where pennies were rolled
down a chute, two boys kept the stallholder talking while 'Skinny'
Belcher pushed a penny on to a lucky number. He could just
manage to get his bony hand under the wire grille. We didn't push
our luck at this particular game too often.

I once had four pennies and four half-pennies to take to the
fair – a whole 6d. The stand that most took my fancy had a fast-
talking man who was selling envelopes, one of which should
contain a watch. It was sixpence a go. I was absolutely fascinated

by the possibility that I might win a watch and after a lot of deliberation, I decided to risk the whole 6d. As I stepped forward with all of my wealth in my hand, a man stopped me and whispered: 'Don't give him the money, luv, it's a con, you'll never win a watch. Go and spend your pennies on the swings'. He obviously meant what he said, and I took his advice. In fact, the swings were the cheapest things at the fair. I had one piece of luck on that occasion for I found a copper on the ground and had a go at throwing three balls in a bucket for a coconut. It must have been a lucky penny as I managed to win a coconut. It seemed so wonderful that I could hardly bear to break it open. Jack smashed it with a stone, however, and shared it out in a dozen dirty pieces. I am sure that it was the best coconut at the fair.

Strangely enough, although our mouths watered at the sight of other people licking their ice creams, eating toffee apples, biting at sticks of rock or tucking into Hot Dogs, we had no feelings of envy for such affluence was beyond our wildest dreams. When we straggled home at the end of the day we all felt that we had had a wonderful time at the fair. I still secretly wonder, though, if I might have won that watch.

In Northam Road, next to Wakes the grocer's, was my favourite shop, kept by a Mr Toefield. We children spent hours looking at the toys and bikes in his windows. The notices on his goods announced that for only sixpence down and a penny a week we might buy some of the smaller items. The grander ones, however, would require a higher deposit and a weekly payment of as much as sixpence. Mr Toefield kept the article until it was paid for – he charged no extra – but he wasn't taking any chances with the more unreliable inhabitants of Northam. With our noses pressed tight against the pane, we knew that we could never afford any of the larger, more expensive toys but felt that there was no harm in just looking. The big window at the front held all the toys and games, the window at the side, all the bikes. It was a wonder that my nose didn't make a hole in the side pane of glass for a bicycle was at the very pinnacle of my dreams. There were two places in Northam where boneshakers could be hired for a small sum and once, when one of my older cousins squandered a whole penny on hiring a bicycle, she was gracious enough to let me have a go at riding the machine. Standing up on the pedals – I couldn't reach the saddle – I was in a transport of delight for the length of the street and then

back again. When I'm grown up and ever so rich, I promised myself,
I'll have that red one in the corner of Mr Toefield's side-window.

V

Uncle Joe, Mum's brother, came to live with us when I was nine
years old. He was a lovely, cheerful man, who was full of fun and a
great worker. He had formerly worked in the docks as a painter and
now he was on the dole like so many other working men. Uncle Joe
had an allotment near the railway bridge and I was his right-hand
man in allotment matters: I was his favourite because I was very
willing to work with him. I planted things as he had shown me,
helped to lift potatoes, weeded and rushed out with a bucket to get
manure from the horses that were kind enough to deposit their
dung in our road and was generally made to feel rather important. I
also went round knocking at doors trying to sell bundles of firewood –
big, generous bundles – which Uncle had previously prepared:
they were two for 1½d. At blackberry-gathering time, Uncle took
me on the bar of his bicycle out to the 'Clump', as it was called, to
pick them, and after a hard day's gathering we would return with
our bags and baskets full. Uncle would put me on a tram with the
blackberries and cycle like fury to keep up with me and his precious
blackberries, so as to be able to help me off at the journey's end. We
then lived like lords on the most marvellous jam which he made
from the blackberries. There was no thought of saving any of the
jam, we just ate until it was all gone. 'Let them enjoy it while they
can,' was a favourite saying of Uncle Joe's.

He did any odd jobs which might bring in a little money. It was
at this difficult time that Uncle found a wallet with £60 and the
owner's address inside, a posh area in Bassett where the nobs
lived. £60 was a small fortune to us and Uncle must have been
sorely tempted to keep it. He could have spent it on essentials like
food and clothing for us. He didn't, but walked all the way to
Bassett to save the tram fare (his bike needed a new tyre) in order
to return the wallet to its rightful owner. He took about an hour to
get there and hoped for some reward for his honesty. He knocked
on the door of the imposing house and asked if he could see the
owner. The maid told him to wait and closed the door. Then, the
door was opened by a gentleman in evening clothes who asked
haughtily, 'What do you want with me, my man?' Uncle asked him

if he had lost a wallet and if so, could he describe it. The man's manner changed immediately – he was now positively beaming. Uncle felt sure that he had done the right thing and certain that he was going to get a handsome tip of money for his effort. The man took the wallet from Uncle's outstretched hand and, with a 'Thank you very much, my man', shut the door in his face. So much for my Uncle's honesty!

Uncle was married but separated from his wife. Mum told me that Uncle's wife got her separation from him on grounds of cruelty. Apparently, Uncle threw something at a mirror and broke it. His wife alleged he threw it at her. She was very houseproud and was always changing the furniture, which they couldn't really afford. I couldn't possibly imagine my Uncle being cruel: he was in my eyes the kindest man in the world. Uncle rarely lost his temper, although when he did it was terrible to see.

A small man, shorter than Mum and younger by two years, his hair was thin and straight, and bright blue eyes adorned a cheerful long face, very like Jack Hulbert's. Uncle adored children – anybody's children. He always had time for us and was Mum's mainstay for many long years. I used to think that there wasn't anything in the world that Uncle Joe couldn't do. He was always working at something or the other. Very occasionally, Uncle would come home with a black eye or a bruised face: he had probably been arguing about politics. His excuse was always the same – he had bumped into a lamp-post. Mum would do her secretive little smile when he said 'I must get that lamp-post moved'. Labour party politics seemed to be the only thing that caused him to get a glint in his eye.

I had plenty of Uncles and Aunties because Mum was one of thirteen children. Two of my Aunts, Kath and Bell, were always at loggerheads. Aunt Kath thought that she was delicate and was always having a touch of the vapours. I used to take her bottle of smelling salts to the chemists to get it refilled with spirits of ammonia which was pungent stuff. We children used to sniff it and get watery eyes to pretend to have an attack of the vapours. We especially liked giving some innocent child a sniff. 'Take a deep breath,' I would say, being the soul of generosity. Aunt Bell was a very down-to-earth person and stood no nonsense when Aunt Kath had one of her attacks. One day when Aunt Kath lay swooning on the carpet Aunt Bell got a full bucket of water and poured it over her face. Aunt Kath jumped up straight away from the floor. Instant recovery! The delicate Aunt Kath never had another attack; at least, not while Aunt Bell was around. Aunt Bell had no children of her own and was always very good to us. One lovely summer's day she and Uncle took us on the bus for a treat to Netley beach. Uncle was longing to have a swim but he was so thin that he was shy about exposing his legs. He was one of the thinnest men I ever saw. 'Go on, luv,' said Auntie, 'keep your long johns on.' And Uncle did! I will always remember that odd figure struggling down to the water in a queer sort of hop-and-jerk movement over that uncomfortable stone beach. He played in the water with us and when he was ready to come out, Auntie waded in up to her knees and wrapped a towel around him to save his blushes.

It was at Aunt Bell's house that I first noticed her lovely margarine so I asked Mum later 'Why can't we have marge like Auntie Bell's, its ever so nice?' I didn't realize that it was butter, not having tasted that before. Mum had to explain the difference between butter and margarine and she then gave us some sugar on our bread-and-marge as a special treat. We thought it was marvellous.

VI

Our house in Radcliffe Road had a tiled front garden and there was a brass door-tread, letterbox and knocker, which were always the first job for Mum who kept them glistening. I was always very proud of our front – even a ragamuffin can feel proud. The front room was on the left as you entered, with the stairs going straight up from the passage. The middle room, with a range for a fireplace, came next and was the room which Mum used to let. Then there was our living room with another range in it, and finally the kitchen. The previous owner had had the lavatory put inside and I was even proud of that. I didn't know anybody else in Northam who had an inside toilet. I had the job of tearing up squares of paper and threading string through a hole in them so that they could hang in the lavatory; tissue paper was especially favoured. The whole reason for my job was because Mum couldn't afford toilet rolls. Many a bottom was dusted with printers ink!

We had three bedrooms upstairs. Once a week, summer and winter, the coal-man dumped one hundred-weight of coal in the cupboard under the stairs and the fine, black dust seemed to be everywhere. Mum bought her coal from the coal-man but many other people went to the Gas Works to buy a sack of coke for sixpence. Any old pram or trolley was used to carry the coke. The entrance to the Gas Works was on the left-hand side of Marine Parade, where two men would put your sack under the chute and load it. I sometimes went with my friend Pat and as one of the men on the chute was her Uncle, she only paid him twopence, which he put in his pocket. Small general shops also sold coal brickettes. They were as laige as a house brick and made out of coal dust. They sold at two for 1½d and one would burn for a long time.

The living-room range was blackened and polished once a week. Mum had a box containing the black-and-yellow tin of *Zebra Grate Polish*, with a 'put-er on' brush and a 'take-er off' one. I wasn't allowed to forget it when I put on with the 'take-er off', and still couldn't understand why I couldn't 'take off' with the 'put-er on'. Two kettles lived permanently on the top of that range. We always had hot water, and loved to toast our bread against the bars on the front. We cooked roast potatoes in the oven, roasted chestnuts on the top, dried washing on a guard around the front – damp boots and shoes would dry overnight on the rack above it.

The only furnishings the kitchen boasted were a black iron gas stove, supplied by the gas company which was then privately-owned, a small table on which Mum kept her pots and pans and a washing bowl, and a gas boiler which stood next to the gas stove. Apart from the kitchen sink and drainer, that was all there was. Two nails on the back door took care of the towels.

It was the living room which was the hub of the home and, as we never owned more than one coat at a time, the door giving access to the living room from the passage accommodated the outdoor clothes for the family. Uncle Joe did have a best suit, it's true, but it was kept upstairs, for high days and holidays. Mum scrubbed the floor every day on her hands and knees, until she had scrubbed the pattern out of the lino, which became a uniformly brown colour. The bread bin, a big white enamel square tin, was large enough for four loaves and that stood on the floor in the corner behind the door with the coats. There was just room next to that for a chair, then came the table with another chair underneath it against the wall and a third chair next to the cupboard by the fireplace. A fourth chair was opposite the one against the wall. There was the contraption, which we called 'Ken's cupboard,' on the other side of the room, and next to that we had a series of old chairs and, for a time, a narrow chaise-longue which somebody hadn't wanted; they stayed under the window. It really was a small room. On the right-hand side of the range were two narrow cupboard doors, the bottom parts of which held shoe-polishing equipment and the Zebra brushes and polish; also firewood and a few tools such as hammer, chopper, pliers and the foot for shoe repairs. The top sections up to the ceiling were divided into three parts, two of which held all the undergarments and clothes for the family, and the third, some twelve inches wide, was Mum's larder. On the lino-covered table which we used for meals, we also played patience, ludo and snakes-and-ladders. Ken did his Meccano and his wood-carving there, and all three of us used it for our drawing and dabbled with our paint boxes. On that invaluable table, Uncle Joe mended the shoes, using his iron cobbler's foot with its three different-sized feet, and Mum used her mincer. Small babies were bathed in a small bath on it and we young children sat on the edge with legs dangling, to have our cuts and bruises tended to. Mum did her ironing and mixed the Christmas pudding on it. Uncle skinned the rabbits and plucked the chickens there; it was also his wallpapering table and his step-ladder. Mum cleaned her brass there, and once a week the knives had a birthday when she rubbed them bright and shiny with knife powder. Small children used it as an indoor house and the cat often sat underneath to keep out of everyone's way. Uncle made his rope mats sitting at the table and Mum mashed up the potato peelings with the bran in a bucket for the chickens. That wonderful table was always in demand: it was the hardest worked piece of furniture in our house.

A tasselled fringe was pinned round the edge of the mantel-piece. Two brass plates on the wall above proclaimed that 'EVERY DARK CLOUD HAS A SILVER LINING' and 'NEVER PUT YOUR WISHBONE WHERE YOUR BACKBONE OUGHT TO BE'. Our house not having a bathroom, it took Mum ages to get through Saturday bath-night. She was a loving soul and warmed our clean underclothes on the oven door for us to wear after the bath. Mum always warmed the towel in which she dried us. The big bath which normally hung on a nail outside was brought in and placed on the mat in front of the fire. The smallest child had the freshest water which was heated on the range in pots, saucepans and kettles. A large knob of common washing soda was put in to soften our hard Southampton water.

More hot was added with each successive child. 'I don't see why they should always go first,' I complained, 'I bet they both pee'd in the bath!' We went to bed as soon as we were bathed. Mum was the last to bath. Uncle Joe used to go to the public baths. Mum would wash the coloured clothes in the bath water. The copper in the kitchen would have been boiling the whites while bath-night went on. Mum would work on till the small hours of the morning until she had finished her washing. Mum let a lady up the road borrow our bath and she, in turn, loaned it to her sister. Suddenly half the kids in our road had the itch! As we got it after the others, Mum wondered if it was due to our bath. We all had to go to the Clinic and have sulphur baths for weeks. Mum never let anyone borrow her bath again. It was very humiliating for her, as she tried so hard to keep us clean.

Uncle Joe kept the house well painted. He used to wear his Cunard coat to bring home paint from the docks. We had Cunard paint all over the house. Our kitchen was the colour of Cunard funnels. I used to ask Mum what a Cunard coat was but she would laugh and still not explain. Clever Uncle Joe used to make rope mats for the house. He would plait long strands of rope and knit them on a huge frame or sew them in fancy patterns. He used a needle about eight inches long which was triangular in section before it finished at a point and he wore a leather pad on his hands called a sailmaker's palm to force the needle through the thickest of material. I was amazed that his coarse and calloused hands, scarred and torn by many a jab from the vicious needle, could make such beautiful mats. Local people were quite willing to buy one of his hard-wearing mats. He would dye strands red or green in Mum's bath, much to her annoyance. Uncle didn't rinse it out properly and Mum would have a pale-green child from the first bathwater.

When Uncle came home one day from work. I thought he looked extra fat – he was usually only a slight man. 'I see you're wearing your Cunard coat again', said Mum, with a smile. 'Oh, please tell me why it is called a Cunard coat,' I begged. It was Uncle's turn to laugh. 'Because I *cun ardly* get it off,' he said to me. Mum helped him off with the coat and there, wound round his body, was a thick coil of hawser rope, stretching from his armpits to the top of his thighs. The mystery of a Cunard coat was now revealed; it was no wonder that he had looked so fat in it. Mum told me that the

A typical house in Northam

rope was off-cuts and of no use to anybody. It was discarded and would have been thrown away.

The people in Northam were poor – with a few exceptions, they were *very* poor – so much so that few doors were locked at night; all people had to offer was themselves, for there was nothing worth stealing. Most homes contained the barest essentials, a table, chairs, bed, frequently with old coats on the top for extra warmth in the winter. There were often four children sleeping in the larger beds.

Northam was dominated by the Gas Works and the wharves, which spread around its edges. This peninsula of Northam was divided from the adjoining district by a railway line on which the coal trucks rattled, banged and were shunted up and down all day and night long. Our house, in common with others on our side of the street, backed on to the railway line.

As well as the ever-present coal-dust, there were bugs and fleas, and Mum, like most of the other women, wore herself to a frazzle fighting these two menaces to our health. When I was at school and was told about the Black Country, I used to think that it surely could not be worse than here at Northam. I used to feel ridiculously proud when at school we undressed for PT because my vest was so white. Mum used to hang the light-coloured things indoors to dry, because if they were put outside they came in blackened. Babies left outside in prams soon got a fine spray of soot and coal particles over their faces. When we walked the pavements, we could feel the crunch, crunch of coal bits under our shoes. The mothers who really tried to keep us kids looking clean deserved a medal for their efforts.

The huge wall next door but one from us, part of a coal dump, was ideal for playing ball against. The only trouble was the dreaded Mrs Ferret, who lived on the other side of that wall. She was a brave child who retrieved her ball from Mrs Ferret's garden. She appeared as from nowhere to give us a ticking off and if she got to the ball first, then that was the end of that ball. She must have spent her life peering through her net curtains in the front bay window, for nothing in the life of the street escaped her eagle eye. Mrs Ferret was also a money-lender, who charged outrageous rates of interest. She took as collateral wedding rings, a man's best boots or suit; and, on one occasion the pension book of an old lady, duly signed on the back so as to cover the amount loaned, together with the interest.

As every street had its resident money-lender, so it had also a wise-woman, who was severally midwife, general practitioner without qualifications, and layer-out of the dead. (You only went to the doctor if you were dying.) My Aunt Flo was a 'wise-woman.' She was a round, brown-faced woman with dark hair and eyes like black twinkling buttons. A strange warmth radiated from her. I suppose her success was partly due to luck, partly to common sense, and something to the lore passed on by my grandmother

who, in her time, had been a street wise-woman. If people then had
had better food I expect that they would have recovered their
health more quickly but, as it was, socks were wrapped around
sore-throats, bricks were heated in the oven and wrapped in cloth
to warm sick people in bed, all at Aunt Flo's direction. Senna Pods
were always part of her stock-in-trade, for she was a firm believer
in the notion that many maladies could be cured by opening the
bowels. If all else failed and the doctor had to be called, neighbours
would lend a sheet and pillow cases, or even a bedspread, to make
things nice for the doctor; he possibly noticed the same bedspread
on different beds.

Pride is a peculiar thing. Adults seem to ignore the fact that
children have eyes and ears and think that children are not aware
of things which are considered to be none of their business. As I
grew older and was sent scurrying for newspapers and a large piece
of thick brown paper, I was well aware that (a) someone was having
a baby or (b) some other mysterious bleeding was going on. The
brown paper went on the mattress first and then the newspaper on
top to soak up the blood and water. Hot water was kept going on
the hob and a towel was put over the rail of the bed for the mother
to pull on during her labour pains. Aunt Flo had no idea how many
babies she had delivered in her long career as midwife. Abortions
were quite common. Slippery Elm, crochet hooks, syringes were
among the few things I can remember being used. Of course
things went wrong at times: Mum nearly died as a result of a
septic abortion, I can remember that she was questioned closely
about it in hospital but these desperate women never gave
away what instrument had been used or who carried out the
abortion.

When Aunt Flo did the laying out for my Uncle Fred, I can
distinctly remember an old stocking wrapped around the jaw to
keep the mouth closed. Later, when the corpse was in the coffin,
all beautifully dressed in a fancy gown and resting on two chairs in
the front room, people were allowed to file slowly past to pay their
last respects, children as well. Aunt Flo had given a final touch to
Uncle Fred before people were admitted. She told me to get the
rouge and some cotton wool from the top of an aspirin bottle.
Delicately, with the touch of a great artist, Aunt Flo put just a
little colour on the cold cheeks. After poking a small piece of
cotton wool up his nostrils – to prevent his pinched expression –

she stood back and said: 'There, though I do say it myself, our Fred looks better now than he has done for a long time'.

Funerals were a great event and all the hard-won pennies that had gone in to death insurance policies came back in to their own. Apart from the cost of the funeral carriage, drawn by fine black horses, the relatives and friends of the deceased probably had sufficient money left over for black clothes. If the purse wouldn't stretch to a black coat for a woman or a black suit for a man then a black arm-band was essential for those who wished to show respect for the dead. After the departed had been decently laid to rest, there were usually ham sandwiches with pickles and cakes and biscuits, with beer for the men and tea for the women of the funeral party. A good send-off for the lost one was deemed to be absolutely essential and many people would rather forego food than miss paying the insurance man the weekly pennies for a death policy insurance. All curtains in the street would be drawn and as the cortege passed by men and small boys together would doff their caps while the women mainly covered their hats and faces with large black veils.

Eldest daughters, of whom I was one, became automatic Cinderellas but I was, however, a very happy one. I didn't mind selling Uncle Joe's bundles of wood, so long as I could keep out of sight of my school friends. If I saw any of them I hid in a doorway until they had passed. I had several regular customers for whom I ran errands. One old lady used to send me to the pawn shop once a month. On one of these trips I was given a vacuum cleaner to pawn which was larger than I was. I lugged it all over the place but none of the pawn-shops were interested in taking it. The old lady was quite cross about it and gave me tuppence for the whole morning's fruitless effort.

At this time there were only three of us children and Mum was our sole support. She drew no widow's pension, and she had no public assistance, other than free meals – breakfast and dinner, five days a week, for us children. At Northam, there was a meals centre for children in dire need. They came from all over Southampton and, if they lived too far out to walk, they were given a blue tram token. Breakfast was at 8.00 a.m. and consisted of half a slice of bread and margarine and half a slice of bread and jam with a mug of cocoa. This was served on Monday, Wednesday and Friday mornings. On the other days, breakfast consisted of a bowl of very thin porridge or watery milk and a slice of bread. Dinners were more varied, with lots of potatoes and minced meat but, unfortunately for most children, there was sometimes Irish stew which they hated because it was so thin and had bits of fat floating on the top. On two days a week there were apples or oranges as extras. given out instead of pudding. This was the highlight of the free meals for many. I think there must have been some two hundred who attended this meals centre. We older girls saw to the 'babies' table at the bottom of the hall before our turn to be served came. The free-meal centre was in Belvedere Terrace, between a bakery and a Chapel. I was fortunate enough to get a job there wiping-up after breakfast and dinner. There seemed to be hundreds of plates and utensils, and probably there were! From the breakfast session I went straight on to school about five minutes away. The school dinner hours were from 12 noon to 2 p.m. so by working as fast as I could, I was able to go home before returning to school, with a jug of soup, a dish of mixed left-overs of dinner or rice pudding, sometimes a quart of milk and one of those extra-long loaves. The two ladies who ran the kitchen never gave me any money but payment in kind was better than cash and Mum was more than grateful. I would leave the food on the table, as Mum would be out at work, and then race back to school. I never thought of myself as hard done by – indeed, the reverse – I thought I was very lucky. I had a marvellous appetite and would eat as much as I could which I feel certain assured good health. Ken and Dorothy were both finicky and could not eat some of the food at the free-meal centre, eating only what they fancied. As for me, I liked everything. Ken was quite healthy but Dorothy was always ailing. Tonsilitis, boils, pleurisy, colds – there always seemed to be something wrong with her. I remember her being desperately ill once and then, as if by magic, grapes and oranges appeared by her bedside. She was too ill to eat them and I, not realizing how very ill she was, was only too happy to oblige. She was breathing with difficulty, the breath whistling through a tiny hole in her throat, swollen with quinsey. Mum was torn between going to work and staying at home with Dorothy: she couldn't afford to stay at home and was afraid to leave her daughter. She went to work but gave Aunt Flo half-a-crown to call the doctor. When he arrived, he sent over to a pub for brandy and sterilized the end of his pair of scissors in the spirit so that he could risk cutting the swelling at the back of her throat. The doctor said that she would not have lasted much longer as she was. Fortunately, Dorothy recovered. Aunt Flo nursed her like the angel she was.

Even I seemed to realize how ill Dorothy really was, though it was the first time I had seen death cast its shadow in our family. Up till then, it had been simply a matter of the occasional bilious attack and growing pains. I was never really surprised to be told that what I was suffering from was growing pains for I was such a tall girl. At eleven I was as tall as any teacher at school, except Miss Evans. School I just about tolerated where English, sports, needlework and art were my favourite lessons. All our teachers were quite strict and it was out of the question for us to cheek them. Miss Evans was the dragon with a capital D. Even the boys from the other side (the school was divided into Boys and Girls) respected her. Miss Evans could lay it on as well as any man and her tongue was pure vinegar. This dreadful, fearsome creature, with her hair drawn back in a tight bun, her large nose stuck on a large ungainly face, had a dual nature. She was an ogre but was also a damned good teacher and we really listened to her because we knew she would not put up with sloppy work. I will always be grateful to her.

It was rather amusing to see a few daring parents cross swords with her over their children. It didn't happen often and they didn't stand a chance with her. She would fix them with her cold eyes and with her tongue like a rapier – her educated voice was never raised – send them away utterly defeated. She gave much of her time to sports which was her big thing. I was among the favoured ones at sports, being especially keen on the high jump and hurdles. I wasn't, however, any good at straight-forward running. A little fat girl was our champion at this and she came in first at the county sports ground competition one year. On arriving at the ground we were suddenly confronted with borrowed, spiked shoes, to be worn that afternoon. Having trained for so long in plimsolls (we used to train in the parks as well as the school playground), this was hopeless for me: they felt all wrong, and I am afraid I did not do very well.

When I was in Miss Evans' class, I had to stay away from school for one whole day. I cannot remember now where I was living but there was a car outside the house with a low luggage rack at the back. When a man got in the car to drive it away I perched precariously on the black iron rails meant for luggage in order to have a free ride. The car went down the road, and turned the corner into the next road which was covered in fresh gravel. We were going faster now and I shouted and banged on the outside for him to stop but he couldn't hear me. So I fell off into the road and was so badly grazed that I had a job to walk home. *Germolene* and bandages were applied to my grazes and I returned to school the following day. When Miss Evans asked me why I was bandaged up, I stupidly told her what had happened. She was a car driver herself and was so angered by my story that she bent me over the brass top guard around the fireplace in the classroom and gave me a stern walloping. 'If I catch any other girls playing such dangerous games, they will get the same treatment!' she told the hushed class.

One day in class I sat sniffing because I had a cold. Miss Evans called me to the front and, in what seemed a ghastly silence, took up a piece of white cotton material and tore a square from it. This was silently handed to me and no further words were required. The sound of the tearing and the embarrassment remained long with me. Shame-faced, I returned to my desk at the rear of the class. I was always at the rear of everything because I was so tall. I was also deaf in one ear from a mastoid, so learning was always more difficult for me.

One day, Dorothy attracted the attention of Miss Evans: she was dirty I suppose, at least her frock must have been. 'How dare you come to school in such a filthy state,' Miss Evans said. 'Look at yourself, tell your mother to wash your dress'. Dorothy, with tears not far away in her voice said 'My Mummy is in hospital'. 'Well, then,' replied Miss Evans, 'tell your father to clean you up before you come here again.' 'My Daddy's dead,' said the small voice. Nothing further needed to be said.

After that, Miss Evans treated my sister and myself with a little more warmth, although she remained as strict as ever for she had no favourites. On two later occasions when Dorothy was ill and away from school, Miss Evans brought fruit of various sorts to our home and wanted to know how Dorothy was. The Christmas following the incident of Dorothy and the dress, Miss Evans called on Mum and gave her tickets for Peter Pan but we were not told that they came from her as she asked Mum to keep it a secret.

I made dreadful mistakes with my English, always saying the

wrong thing at the wrong time. Some visiting Nuns came to our class-room and asked what we could tell them about the Octopus. My hand shot up and waved eagerly to attract the questioner's attention. I did so and she asked 'You there at the back?'. I replied: 'Please Miss, the Octopus has eight testicles'. I couldn't understand her strange smile at my answer. Another time, at Cookery class (I had only just started), the teacher said, 'Now, I want you girls, all on your own, and without any help from me to make the cheapest meal for four that you can'. This was child's play, or so I thought. I mixed something like a pound of flour with water into a dough-like mixture, which I then fried in four round lumps. I put a little sauce on the top of each lump. 'What on earth is that?' the teacher asked. 'Please miss,' I replied, 'it is a hot, filling meal for four'. As we had often eaten this at home, I didn't think it strange and was puzzled by her looks of astonishment.

VII

Sadie, my friend from our road, was not just a friend but more a soul-mate. We did all sorts of exciting things together. Once, we wanted to see the silent lantern-show at the Central Hall but didn't have enough money to get in. So we walked in a side-door during the afternoon and hung about till evening when we saw the show free. We also thought up the idea of getting on one of the Green Buses and hiding under the seats upstairs. If we were caught, we would say that we had lost our money. To our delight, we travelled all the way to Salisbury, 20 miles away, under the seat before we were discovered. The bus conductor was not impressed by our story of lost money, even if we thought ourselves as budding actresses. He did, however, let us stay on the bus until it turned round, as he put it, and we came all the way back to Southampton, this time sitting on a seat.

We only played truant once; the School Board man was too sharp for us in those days. One day only was allowed for being absent from school and after that a visit was paid to the child's parents. On this occasion, we infiltrated the nearby district of Central and made up two lovely bunches of flowers which we took from other people's gardens. These we gave to our Mums saying that they were presents from the other girl's garden. Our Mums were so pleased with them that we repeated the performance. 'Here you are, Mum', I said. 'Some more flowers from Sadie's garden. Her Mum sent them for you'. Sadie told the same story. Eventually, Mum and Sadie's Mum met, and there were mutual thanks expressed for the bouquet from the other's garden. As neither of them grew such rare blooms, we were unmasked and duly walloped.

Sadie and I hit on the idea of mixing dried horse manure with dog-ends picked up from the gutters, putting them in tins, and most considerately handing them to any poor old man we might come upon. We had a splendid refinement on the game of knocking on doors at night and running away, which we called 'ghost tapping'. A piece of black cotton, with a button fixed 6 inches from the end, would be fixed by a drawing-pin just above a window; which had to be a front window, with a light on, for someone had to be at home to hear the 'ghost tapping'. From the other side of the button the black cotton would stretch right across the road to where we would be hiding behind a hedge. By a gentle jerking of the invisible thread, a tapping sound would be made on the opposite window. People would open their front doors and find no-one there. The more often they opened their doors, the more we would giggle and snigger, concealed on our haunches behind the hedge.

The boys had one particularly nasty game. A new arrival to the road would hang around on the edge of a gang of children, obviously eager to join in the fun. The bigger boys would send one of us over to ask the newcomer if he wanted to join our gang. From eagerness to join, or possibly fear of what the consequences might be if he refused, the 'victim' usually agreed to the terms offered. 'Do you want to be in with our lot?' he would be asked. 'If so, you must become a Knight of the Golden Sword'. 'How do I become a Knight of the Golden Sword?' the victim would reply. Then the explaining would begin. First, he was to get a piece of rag or a large hankie for binding across his eyes. Then he would kneel and firmly grasp the Golden Sword with two hands. Three times he was to say 'I am a Knight of the Golden Sword' in a loud voice, and he would touch his forehead on the sword-hilt each time he repeated the special phrase. When all had been explained, a sword was made from two bits of wood, the hilt being tied on with string. The victim was blindfolded and made to kneel eager to say the sacred words. While the sword was being made, some of the children would search for dog's mess, the runnier the better. As soon as the victim's eyes were covered, the sword-hilt was smeared with the dog's mess and the gang leader would hand him the weapon (by the blade). I laughed as much as anyone when he took it and repeated the 'I am the Knight' phrase, by the time that he had touched his forehead three times, we had all run away convulsed with laughter. I wonder why I laughed when I thought it such an awful trick.

Another silly game we played was 'parcel on a string' which was best played at night. We made up a parcel, and left it temptingly on the pavement by the 'cut'. We then hid up the 'cut'. Hardly anybody can resist picking up something they think they have found. Some people even looked craftily round before stooping to examine it. The moment the inquisitive person bent down, we would jerk the parcel away with our piece of string. One of us was always made look-out-man and the game could be played for hours on end.

Poor Sadie got all the blame for our escapades. Mum couldn't stand her, and she was the only person I can remember who had to wait outside the front door for me. Mum just wouldn't let her into the house. Sadie's Mum blamed me as being the one who had led her Sadie astray, but she still let me into her house. Sadie was an only child and seemed lonely without my company. I used to pray that the boy who lived next door to Sadie was not around when I called for her. He always used to call out, 'Nancy, tickle your fancy, oh my charming Billy Boy.' I hated him.

I played so often with Sadie that I am afraid I sometimes neglected my sister Dorothy. She was always begging to come with us, and from my superior position of being two years older I would tell her to 'Go away, we don't want kids with us.' But at night, when we were in bed, I used to make up stories for her and she would not go to sleep until I had told her one. Some of the girls of my age liked to push babies out in prams but if they called for me with somebody's baby in a pram I always told them: 'I've had enough of kids; if you're taking that out you can go without me!'

Saturday-morning matinées at the cinema filled my silly head with stage romance. I saw some of the shows at the Palace and Hippodrome but only on very rare occasions. One such was when Uncle Joe took us for a very special treat. I can remember him getting the metal discs with a hole in them at the back entrance of the theatre; these discs were in place of tickets. We then climbed lots of stairs to get to the top of the theatre. We were going up into the 'Gods', as it was then called. On arrival, a man there would take the metal disc and place it on a spike. There were no individual seats in the Gods, just rows of steps as in a Roman Amphitheatre. If we could, we would get a seat in the middle at the very front. From there Dorothy and myself would be able to see the man working the spot-lights for the artists on the stage. He would slide coloured glass plates in front of the beam of light; I used to wonder how he knew which colour was which in the semi-gloom. I saw some of the famous stars, Harry Lauder, the Houston Sisters – Renée and Billy, and Teddy Brown and his xylophone. There were snake charmers, contortionists, magicians, Egyptian sand dancers with funny long shoes, singers and jugglers. But, most of all, it was the pretty young dancers of the chorus whom I loved to watch and I came back from these shows starry-eyed with my head in the clouds. I knew exactly what I wanted to be when I grew up – a film dancing star! Dorothy and I worked hard to imitate the stars. I could dance like Shirley Temple, drawl in a husky voice 'I want to be alone' like Greta Garbo, and take off Jimmy 'Snozzle' Durante. What I had to have was a pair of tap-dancing shoes and clever Uncle Joe fixed me up with a pair. He cut out some pieces of heavy zinc and screwed them on the toes and heels of my shoes. I was thrilled with them. I tapped and clicked my way all over the house, on the pavement, on the way to school next morning, and even tapped all the way up the stairs to my class-room. I tried to make my tapping as quiet as possible when in school but I really let myself go in the playground. My teacher was not amused. 'Do *not* come to school with those shoes on this afternoon,' I was told. 'Please miss,' I replied, 'they are the only shoes I have, Uncle made them for me.' 'Then get Uncle to unmake them for you.' 'But I shan't see him till tonight,' I whimpered. 'Very well then, get them fixed tonight, but do not come here in the morning unless you have!' was her final crushing comment. I decided that I would not mention this conversation when I got home and that if I walked very quietly my teacher would not hear my tap-shoes. I tapped my way home and into the house, and then up the stairs into the bed-room and downstairs again – by which time Mum had had enough. My floods of tears did not stop her from getting Uncle to take the offending taps off my shoes. Just like grown-ups, I thought.

Sadie and I made up our own concerts and one day she begged

me to show her parents how I could cross my feet around the back of my neck – the supreme party-piece of my contortion act, which consisted of standing on my head, on my hands, walking on my hands, doing the Russian splits, and then the crab walk, etc.

Sadie arranged for me to go round to her house. In the living room her Mum and Dad sat on two chairs facing me, as I took up my position on the floor. Slowly and gracefully, from a sitting posture, I raised my left leg and put it round the back of my neck. Balancing on my bottom, I then, equally gracefully, slowly raised my right leg. As I did so, I broke wind, in a strangled sort of long drawn-out noise. My act was ruined. Sadie's parents laughed until they cried. I didn't complete my act as we were all too convulsed with laughter. Her parents pulled my leg for years after and whenever I was in their house, if anybody made a smell they would look straight at me and ask: 'Have you been putting your feet round your neck again Nance?'

I was always having trouble with my shoes. When I was very small I was given a pair of second-hand boots with black, patent pointed toes and hooks up the front for the laces. They must have come out of the Ark. I could only have been about five but I hated them with all of my heart because they were so ugly. I can remember screaming and struggling as they were put on my feet. I didn't win the unequal struggle and had to give in, after getting many slaps from Aunty, for Mum had already gone to work. Some of the other little girls in my class wore black patent ankle-strap shoes, which were so pretty. Why couldn't I have shoes like that I was always asking. On another occasion when I was a little older the Poor Relief supplied Mum with a docket to get me some shoes. These shoes were great brown, ugly lumpy lace-ups – I hated them as well. I did my best to wear them out, walking through all the puddles and gutters of water that I could find. I tried to kick them to death by scuffling along the ground and kicking out at walls. I managed it in the end. The Poor Relief couldn't understand how such a stout pair of shoes had deteriorated so quickly. They supplied another pair which I let grow old naturally. Uncle Joe came to the rescue when Mum was at her wit's end for money and couldn't afford shoe repairs. He found an old bicycle saddle, made of leather, which he soaked all night and then with a hammer flattened the softened hide. He did a marvellous job in repairing my shoes. The soles and heels that he cut from the saddle were so tough that they even outlasted the uppers.

It was about this time that I was lucky enough to join a concert party called 'The Juvenile Entertainers of Southampton'. We entertained at Working Men's Clubs, hospitals and the 'Home of Recovery'. It did not last long but it was a memorable time of my life. One of the other mums made me a white satin three-piece – top, pants, and skirt – for my contortionist act, free of charge. People one hardly knew could be so kind. I didn't need any shoes for my act. I couldn't get in on the Tap Dancing because I had no tap-shoes. I could do an Hawaiian dance, though: no shoes were needed for that but only a grass skirt. Lovely Uncle Joe made me one. He got some raffia from somewhere and sewed it with his big needle on to a crude brown bodice made from sacking. The hoop of flowers for my neck, and the blossom for my hair were made from crepe paper. But how on earth was I to be made to look like a dusky maiden? Uncle Joe mixed some cocoa in water to form a gritty paste, and told me to rub it on my face when I got to the 'dressing room'. We seldom had a proper dressing room in the places where we performed. The hula-hula dance came long after my contortion act so I didn't get any cocoa on my white satin three-piece. Uncle Joe said that nobody from the audience could tell that my lovely, brown colour came out of a tin of Cadbury's cocoa!

Dorothy, who had a pleasant voice, started to sing at these concerts. She continued long after I had left the concert party, because by then I was separated from her as I was living with another family and couldn't be spared the time. Dorothy was still singing in clubs when she was sixteen. I mercilessly pulled her leg about her singing, and she dared me to come and listen to her singing in the Workmen's Hall, a Labour Club in the district of Chapel. She really could sing and I never pulled her leg again.

Dorothy and I were always singing in the house, except when her throat was bad, and I probably made enough noise for the two of us. Gracie Fields was one of the singers we most liked to take-off. We bawled 'The Biggest Aspidistra in the World' all over the house and tortured the neighbours with our high notes. About this time, I learnt the best song of all, in my opinion – 'Oh for the Wings of a Dove'. I sang it high; I sang it low; I was always singing it.

The woman next door did complain to Mum. I was warbling away upstairs, in front of a looking glass, when Mum rudely interrupted: 'That bird is dead,' she said. 'What bird?' I asked. 'That blasted dove, it's just died of old age' was her crushing reply. Its funny how grown-ups always spoil children's pleasure. When I told Uncle Joe about it he said 'Well, you've got to think of the neighbours, luv!' To cheer me up, he would do the sailor's hornpipe, his party-piece; and we could never get enough of it. His jolly face would be wreathed in smiles as he jiggled up and down in our living room.

I used to hate singing with our music teacher, Miss Lander, as I had a dreadful voice when compared to Dorothy's. Miss Lander was always trying to get me to sing solo: 'Surely you can sing as well as your sister?' was her favourite comment. I often excused myself by saying that I had a sore throat, and couldn't possibly manage to sing. I never had a sore throat in my life; it was poor Dorothy that was always having them. Lying made me feel rather guilty but I just wouldn't sing for Miss Lander. I didn't mind singing 'Nymphs and Shepherds come away, come away' with all the rest of the class, but I could never get the hang of all those quavers, semi-quavers, and treble clefs. Once I drew a picture of Miss Lander, with the words coming out of her mouth in a balloon: 'Do, ray, me, fa, so, la, te, do' and was startled when she told me to 'Bring your work to my desk, girl'. She was really a very nice teacher and didn't make too much fuss about my picture. I had to write out so many times 'I must pay attention when in class'. She wrote on my report: 'Capable of much better work, day-dreams, and talks too much.' Most of the other comments were: 'Talks too much; could do better if she tried harder'; or 'Talks too much; very disappointing results, could do much better if she tried harder'. One report was so bad that I took it home and signed it myself before taking it back, which saved a great deal of bother.

I was always being told that schooldays were the happiest days of my life but I, strongly disagreed with that statement at times. I was longing for the day when I could leave, and go out to work to earn some money. It wasn't so much that I disliked school as that I found it very boring. I couldn't run errands for cash while I was sitting at a school desk. I always thought it most unfair that girls were not allowed to do a paper round which was the most lucrative job for out of school hours. Once when I applied for a paper-boy's job, I was told 'You're not a boy'. 'I know I'm not, but I would be as good as a boy if you gave me a chance,' I reasonably replied. He wasn't having it though: it was my first try at attempting to promote equal opportunity for both sexes.

Miss Getty took us for Religious Instruction: she was a little, dried-up, grey-haired lady, and a very strict teacher. We had to mind our 'P's' and 'Q's' in her class. She took her subject very seriously and impressed upon us an awful God of retribution. Each in turn, we had to read so many lines from the Bible, and it was while we were reading from the second book of Kings that my turn came to read Verse 27, Chapter 18. Miss Getty fixed me with her steely-grey eyes – the same colour as her steely-grey hair. 'You may leave out the next few lines,' she said. The verse contained the following: '. . . that they may eat their own dung, and drink their own piss with you?' It was just too much for my rather unholy sense of humour. I looked at my friend Barbara, sitting next to me, who gave a sort of half-smile. I fought hard not to smile in response. She gave a little snigger and, notwithstanding all my efforts, I felt my chest heave and *I* began to snigger. A rising tide of mirth started in the back of my throat and the next thing I knew was that I was engulfed in laughter and my sides were aching. The whole class was now laughing. Miss Getty was furious with me, and when she had restored order in the classroom, I was sent to wait outside the headmistress's room until I was summoned. I received from her several whacks across the knuckles with a ruler, and was returned to the classroom. Miss Getty was the only teacher who gave the children in her class a Christmas present. She bought one present in each week of the year. When I was in her class, I received my present along with the rest of the class, but I wondered if she would rather have left me out. She treated me with cold correctness after this Bible-reading incident.

Another thing that stands out in my memory about school was when the Clinic sent nurses to inspect our hair for fleas and nits. We were made to file past them and a pencil was used to part our hair. I was always lucky in not having that tell-tale pink slip of paper handed to me. The paper made plain to the whole class that the unlucky recipient had to attend the Clinic for treatment.

Mum, being the soul of cleanliness, kept a vigilant eye on us children. In spite of this, we got fleas in our hair at times. The remedy was Oil of Sassafros: a strong, pungent, burning medicinal oil which made your eyes run if you were unlucky enough to wriggle and some got in them. A paper would be spread on the table, we would be bent over it, standing on a chair if too small, and a very fine-toothed comb pulled through one's hair. That is why 'A fine toothed comb, please' was often asked for at the Chemists. The large fleas would fall on the paper and were then cracked by the back of the thumbnail. The nits had to be pulled off by the finger nails and it took a week, or more, of daily inspections before one's head was finally free of them; three heads took up a lot of Mum's time. It was one of those things that every child occasionally got and which nobody liked admitting to having.

It was the same thing with the bugs: all one could do was to try to keep down the pests in one's own house. I remember Mum being very cross with me because I squashed some on a bedroom wall and made the wallpaper messy. The thing to do was to knock them off on to a piece of paper and then kill them. Bugs were a dirty, dried, blood red colour, similar in size to a ladybird, but flatter. Throughout my childhood, I can't recall anyone who bought a new bed. For most people, beds were bought second-hand. The uninvited guests came when the bed was bought and went when the bed was sold.

I helped Uncle Joe to use a blow-lamp on some iron bedsteads that we had, one hot summer, when the bugs were always at their worst. I don't suppose Uncle or Mum enjoyed it much. Uncle was muttering, 'We'll burn the ruddy things out' – he never used real swear words – but I found such big-game hunting great fun. The flame was directed to the corner joints of the bed, one of the breeding areas of bugs. Young bugs were a whitish version of the adult but much smaller. They weren't so white, however, by the time they had had their fill of us. Unfortunately, if you were bitten during the night you had a nasty red weal in the morning to show for it.

We also had our share of mice in the house and an occasional rat. Trixy was the name of our male tabby cat, whom we all adored. He was never given any food and there weren't any scraps left over for him to have, so he had to work for his living. He lived to a great age which shows that it couldn't have done him any harm. Even Mum was a dab hand at killing mice. There were so many of them in the house that they would become over-venturesome and come out while we were in the room. Mum would snatch up a poker from the fireside and, in a flash, whack one of them dead as it darted in front of the hearth. We were all very proud of Mum's skill.

Rats were a source of sport for another section of Southampton people. I was staying with one of my countless 'Aunties' who owned a shop near St Michael's Church in Holy Road. Mum was then working in St Michael's Lodging house. I stayed with her for quite a while but I cannot remember for how long. There is, however, indelibly imprinted on my mind a picture of the huge rat cages in the basement, as big as parrot cages. In that old part of the town, which was near the water, rats abounded. Mum said that passages ran underneath the centuries-old roads and houses. Three cages in my Auntie's basement imprisoned three rats. They were sleek, with bright glittering eyes and enormous tails, and they moved and squeaked incessantly. These rats were to be part of the week-end sport. Other people were catching rats and similarly keeping them for the same occasion.

St Michael's Square was to be the stadium. This Square was about 40 yards wide and its four sides were flanked by St Michael's Church, St Michael's Lodging House, St Joseph's School, and a row of houses and shops. Standing in the centre of the square were some ten men, all with rats in cages. They formed the first circle with the cages. In front of them, about six yards further away was another circle with a larger number of men, all of them with dogs on a leash, surrounding the cages. The dogs were of every size and colour and were all barking and straining at their leashes to get at the rats. The third, and outer, circle consisted of men, women and children, the boys among them carrying sticks. A subdued excitement filled the air. Voices were raised in suspense. Everyone was waiting for the word 'go'. Above the noise of the dogs and the crowd a man's voice could be heard asking if they were ready, and there was then a sudden hush. The dog-owners crouched over their dogs, eager to release them from their leashes, while the men in the innermost circle bent over the cages ready to open the doors. 'We will count to ten.' 'Are you ready?' Silence. One, Two, Three. As the numbers were spoken, the tension became almost unbearable. 'Ten' was shouted in a triumphant voice. Then the rats were out of the cages and the dogs were off their leashes. The savage spectacle of dogs killing rats then followed. There were three times as many dogs as rats. Any rat that had run the gauntlet and escaped into the crowd was manfully attacked by the boys of the outer circle with their sticks. Women and girls raised their skirts and shrieked. Men laughed in a superior fashion. Children jumped up and down with excitement. It was pure bedlam. Then it was suddenly all over. The weekend sport was finished until the next time.

One block away from St Michael's Square was Holy Rood Church, in the High Street – below Bargate. The street was really wide and very long, being the main arterial route through Southampton. On New Year's Eve it would change its name and become simply, the Asphalt. Dancing on the Asphalt was a time-honoured tradition that took place each year. This ritual attracted people from all over town, from teenagers to the elderly, many of whom visited pubs along the route. Between Holy Rood Church and the Bargate the Asphalt would be packed with people, the overflow spilling into the side roads. It wasn't so much dancing that took place as one boozy, boisterous party. At the stroke of twelve, the bells would peal, and complete strangers would join hands and bawl out the words of 'Auld Lange Syne'. After embracing and wishing each other a 'Happy New Year', they would then sing and dance the hours away. Exhausted, or sobering up, the crowds would gradually disperse and quiet would reign once more. I begged to be allowed to go to the Asphalt when I was older but my request was always firmly refused. Mum did not drink and, besides, she hinted that things sometimes got a 'bit out of hand': it was, to her way of thinking, 'not a nice place to be'.

Politics in Northam, for the children at least, started with the local elections. Northam was fiercely Labour – the Conservatives hadn't a hope there. At each election the Tories put up the same candidate, a Mr Grand, who received very few votes. Huge banners stretching across the width of a street would head a procession comprising a sprinkling of adults and as many as a hundred of us children. We would thoroughly enjoy ourselves, marching up and down the streets of Northam, banging home-made drums and singing at the top of our voices. We sang the same song over and over again; we never tired of singing it on our marches. The song ran:

> 'Vote Vote Vote for Mr Watsit
> Knock old Grandee out the door
> If it wasn't for his wife
> We would stab him with a knife

And they won't vote for Grandee anymore.
Glory Glory Hallelujah!
Teacher hit me with a ruler
Glory Glory Hallelujah!

And my soul goes marching on.
Vote Vote Vote for Mr Watsit
Watsit is the man for me.
Vote for Watsit, he's the man
And We'll have him if we can
And we won't vote for Grandee any more!'

Uncle Joe used to take me to the Common to hear the Fascist Blackshirts. A group of men wearing coloured shirts, would there harangue the listening crowd.

Although I was only a child, I think Uncle used to enjoy having me as his captive audience. He would tell me about how different things were going to be when I grew up, working class people were going to change the social face of England, there would be enough for all to eat, there would be no unemployment. All the rich people, he maintained, would be made to share their wealth with the poor. The sick and needy would receive immediate attention. No-one need ever again to be afraid to call a doctor because they couldn't afford it. 'Things were already changing,' Uncle would insist. 'Why, up in London, they even have a box with a little live picture in it. Its like going to the pictures except that the picture is post-card size. It is called television'.

I remember two men arguing at a political meeting. 'The poor are always with us, mate, and do you know why the poor are always with us?' one of them asked. 'Because they piss their money up against the wall in the pub', retorted the other. We had more pubs in Northam than in other districts of Southampton. It seemed to me as if there were pubs on every other corner. They included: The Ship Inn, the Prince of Wales, the Wonder Inn, the Whites Home, the Falcon Inn, the Cornmotors Arms, the Odd Fellows Arms, the Boiler Makers Arms, the Uncle Tom's Cabin, the Coopers Arms, the Duke of York, and Rose Bud, the Sovereign, the Belvedere, the Jubilee, the Yacht Tavern, the St Leonards, the Northam Inn, the Engineers Arms, the Welcome Home, the

Magdella, the Standard of Freedom and, for good measure, the Off Licence in Northam Road, Evans Liberal Club in Belvedere Terrace and the Conservative Club, also in Northam Road. As the entire male population when I was a child was only 5,056, and that included the newly born as well as the old, it was obvious that those who wanted a drink didn't have far to walk. Women did not generally frequent them, although a child might sometimes be seen outside waiting for its parents. It was always one of my dreams that I, too, might wait outside and get a packet of crisps and a fizzy lemonade. I thought this would be marvellous, but it never happened. The man of the house was very much in charge then and it was accepted that they had the meat and the best of whatever was going, for they were the breadwinners; it was a stark, bald fact, and nobody thought it strange.

Gang fights sometimes occurred between districts with but little provocation. It was usually Central versus Northam or Chapel versus Northam. The tribal instinct was a fanatically strong one: if boys from another district invaded our territory, retaliation swiftly followed. The news of the invasion would spread with the speed of an African bush telegraph. Boys would arm themselves with catapults, sticks, stones, and would use dustbin lids as shields. I always wanted to go with the boys but would be brusquely sent back by Ken. He didn't want any silly young girl hanging around in time of war. I expect there was more noise than actual fighting but 'honour was honour' and our Northam boys were proud of their tradition. Their fathers had fought similar battles in the past with boat-oars and boots as weapons. The police were tough, and showed little hesitation in laying into the bigger boys with their belts to break up the fighting. We had one super-tough policeman in our Northam district but the parents of children chastised by him didn't go wailing to the Authorities. They took their punishment like men and had no resentment for the police; indeed, they respected them. Parents would ask a friendly copper to have a word with their children if it was thought at all necessary. Children got away with what ever they could in the way they behaved – it simply was that we didn't get away with very much! Bigger families meant stricter discipline: there was only one 'Heap Big-Chief' in a family – the rest were Indians!

VIII

Because we needed the money, we shared our home with many lodgers. Mum never wanted to let rooms but she had little choice. First, we had Aunty Bess and Uncle Phil. Aunty Bess was always bright and gay and laughed a lot. Uncle Phil had his moments but was generally rather crotchety. When we all had tea in Aunty's room, especially on her birthday, it was quite a job to seat Mum and us children around the little table. We children were having a lovely giggly time and were getting on Uncle's nerves. 'I've just about had enough of you sniggering, giggling kids,' he grumpily exclaimed. 'The next one to giggle leaves the table!' Mum and Aunt Bess looked at each other and then both started to giggle. We followed suit and Uncle left the room in disgust.

Then there was a very old man who had our best front room. There was nothing remarkable about him except that he cleaned Mum's nice oxidized fire-guard with ashes and rubbed all the shine off. He cleaned the highly polished chiffonier with strong soda-water and left it dull and smeary. He washed the floor and was too old to mop up the water. But, for all that, he was a nice old gentleman. Mum never grumbled because he tried so hard to be clean, and she nursed him in his final illness.

A young married couple with two babies followed the old man. The babies did their share of crying and there were nappies all over the place. Mum was ill and in hospital at one point during their stay and I can remember Aunty Flo saying to the mother 'Perhaps you would be good enough to keep an eye on them,' meaning myself, Ken and Dorothy. She looked at me and said to Aunty: 'They are old enough, and ugly enough, to look after themselves'. The couple didn't stay long and were followed, as I remember, by Bill.

Bill was a little, old, thin man. A sandy-haired beer drinker, with a damp, droopy moustache. He wet his bed and, on most Friday and Saturday nights, returned to his room amiably drunk. He must have rather fancied Mum, because one night when I was going past his room on the way up to bed, he stopped me and asked in a boozy voice. 'How would you like me to be your new Daddy?' I can remember that his gingery moustache was all wet and nasty. I knew Mum didn't much like him. Every Sunday morning he would go to church, and he regularly went to Confession. Mum told me that he asked God to forgive him for wetting the bed and drinking. Bill had to go because he began to pester Mum. After he left, she had to burn his mattress.

The gutters running with rain-water were a source of constant delight to us. We raced boats made of matchboxes and specially folded, hard paper, on the miniature swollen rivers and rushed along with them. How often did we get a clump for coming home with wet shoes and wet sleeves! But what child isn't above such mundane things, when they have lived in a world of pirates, shipwrecks and collisions on the high seas!

The water surrounding the edges of Northam made it in to our 'Riviera'. Groups of children, generally from the same street, would go to the wharves, or near to the Old Northam bridge to swim. Or go to where pieces of wood – twenty feet long – were joined together with rope to form a floating platform. These pieces of wood were soaked in the river as part of the process of seasoning and they made marvellous diving boards!

We had a very wide choice of resorts to go to on sunny days. Shoeless – for this would save wear-and-tear – and dressed in a motley collection of drawers, one leg up and one leg down, off we children would go. Babies came in prams, toddlers toddled – they came in all sizes – with older and very bossy girls in charge of them, some of them being as ancient as twelve or thirteen. I believe the little ones learned to swim almost by accident, as they were left at the water's edge whilst the older ones showed-off out of their own depth.

One affluent young man brought a well patched inner-tube with him on one such expedition. This was most unusual because there were not many cars around in the 1930s – let alone spare inner-tubes. For that day, the 'inner tube' boy was king. Our Northam boys always did well in the School Swimming Galas. The older boys sometimes dived off the top of Northam Bridge into the river. This was a very dangerous thing to do as the currents at that point were treacherous. But boys will be boys, and even the odd drowning would not stop them. Mum's young cousin had been drowned there as a boy.

My own piece of remarkable diving was done from the floating deal logs; I had forgotten that the tide was going out. I came up covered in black, oozing mud which took a lot of getting off, and had a vile taste! If just two or three logs were joined together, they would rock in a crazy way and to walk out on them before diving became part of the daring, the growing-up, and the showing-off.

Sometimes, in the same large groups, we would set off for distant horizons, on expeditions to Netley – eight miles away – where there was a proper beach. The boys would make a trolley – a soap-box on wheels – which was a much admired feat of engineering. An old pram chassis and some pieces of wood would be transformed into a chariot and willing hands pushed from the back for many a mile. A ha'penny's worth of lemonade-powder made several bottles of drink which, together with plain bread and 'marge' as 'eats' – some lucky ones might even have had jam as well – made up our beach picnic and was not any-the-less enjoyed for being simple fare. Such an excursion would be planned and discussed for days beforehand. It took us several hours to get to and back from Netley; it was often dusk by the time we got home.

Netley was just somewhere different; it even smelt quite salty! The stones on the beach were very ordinary but, to a child, their lovely colours were enchanting and of course the stones with holes in them were considered to be very lucky for the finder. The seaweed we made go pop. Sea-gulls had whiter plumage, and their screams were louder and more dramatic than the birds we saw flying over Northam. Wonderful things were to be found in the sea. Sea anenomes, periwinkles, crabs, all sorts of seaweed, and especially the lovely shells. We would gaze in wonder at the lovely mother-of-pearl colour of the inside of a mussel shell. We always collected winkles to take home, a delicacy to be enjoyed the following day.

Young legs that had hopped and skipped to Netley in the morning were weary at the end of a long and exciting day by the sea. We were quite hardy, and it was only the very small ones who had a turn at riding in the box-on-wheels. We older ones might give our younger brothers or sisters a piggyback to help them on the long journey home.

Then, at other times, we would go to the Common, some four miles away, or to Hedge End which was a little further out. We thought of this as 'going to the country' but we followed the same procedure as when going to the sea. Trees and grass were a joy on their own. Someone had the brilliant idea of making our own tents for our country trip. Some of us thought that they could get hold of old sacks, others that they might get bits of old canvas or sheet, and I had a sudden vision of Mum's blue bedspread with the fringe of shiny blue tassles becoming a tent fit for any Sheikh of Arabia. Mum was at work so there was no difficulty in taking the bedspread. On our arrival in the country we all set to, building such palaces as we could with the materials at hand. Branches were broken from bushes or trees to make uprights and stones were used as hammers to bang in the pegs which held our tents to the earth. I felt vaguely uneasy as the corners of Mum's bedspread were fixed to the ground. For the time being, however, I was very pleased with my tent. The boys lit a fire with bits of dead wood and everything seemed to be going with a swing.

We then decided to cross a stream and scrump some apples from an orchard on the other side. A fence had to be climbed to gain entrance but seven of us got over it. We were happily filling our shirts and jumpers with apples. One girl put them in her knickers as she had nowhere else to stuff them when a cry rang out, 'Dogs! Run!' We all managed to get back over the fence except Jenny, a friend's little sister. As she was clambering over, a dog nipped her at the back of the ankle and her shoe was pulled off. Instead of climbing down, Jenny fell and rolled and bumped her way over the embankment down into the stream. She was whimpering and limped back all wet and dirty to our camp. There was more trouble in the form of a large, irate man, who was stamping out the camp fire. He then seemed to do a madman's dance, which involved the kicking down of our motley collection of tents. There could be no doubt that he was the Lord of this particular piece of earth on which we camped. 'Bloody kids,' he shouted, 'Clear off or you'll get my boot up your backsides!' We all hurriedly gathered up our stuff while poor little Jenny stood, wet dripping from the hem of her dress and the tears from her eyes making two clean channels down her mud-daubed face. One of the elders of our tribe kindly suggested that she might be given a lift on the trolley. 'What,' exclaimed another, 'She'll make our Mum's sheet all wet and dirty!' This protest was declared out of order and the wet, muddy and half-shod Jenny was allowed to ride back to civilization and Northam perched precariously on top of all of our junk. It was getting quite dark when we were only a mile or so from home and were going down a long, sloping road. The trolley-cart sped away from us and went careering on with Jenny still perched on the top.

It crashed off the pavement, a wheel came off, and Jenny sailed through the air and landed in the road.

Our stuff was all over the place. The trolley-cart was on its side, three wheels spinning in the air. The fourth wheel lay all buckled up, a couple of yards further on. Poor little Jenny was badly grazed from her thigh to her knee. Her hands were also cut and there was a large bump rising rapidly on her forehead. While we girls clucked around her making suitably sympathetic noises, the boys tried to repair the damaged vehicle. But they had no luck. The battered thing was dragged the rest of the way home with our gear alternately shaken off and returned to the now stricken trolley. Jenny was given piggybacks by a friend and myself. By the time we were over Northam Railway Bridge – and on the very last leg of our homeward journey – it was dark and the gas lamps were alight at the street corners. There, at the top of Britannia Road, stood a group of Mums and Dads. We were each greeted in different ways: 'Come here, you little bugger!' 'Wait till your father lays hands on you' ''Ave you got my sheet, you sod!' Etc. Slaps, whacks, and thuds were intermingled with oows, ows and OUCHES, as the angry parents chastised their children. Fate had not yet dealt its final blow for poor Jenny. For by now the large bump on her forehead, and her continual crying, had closed her eyes into mere slits. She had a distinctly oriental look, more like a refuge from the Chinese border, than a child returning from the country. Holding up her arms to her mother, the one person in the world to whom she could turn for comfort, Jenny wailed 'Mummy'. Her mother looked at Jenny with astonished bewilderment, and half-hugging and half-shaking her, in a voice that was almost hysterical, she screamed: 'What did you want to get yourself in such a state for?' This was the last straw for the poor little bundle of misery who, with renewed vigour, bawled at the top of her voice as she was carried away. I too, of course, had to receive punishment for my ill-treatment of Mum's bedspread. Perversely, as is the way of children, we got more pleasure out of talking about this outing which had ended in disaster than we did of all the others which hadn't.

For the children from our part of Northam, Britannia Road was a very important place. It was extra-long and extra-wide, with a very smooth surface. One entire side of the road was taken up by the Gas Works while the other side had three streets leading off with a main road at each end. There were not many motor cars about in those years, as I have said, nearly all goods being horse-drawn. Britannia Road then was for us children a marvellous open space for hoops and tops. Hoops were made from a ring of iron, or laminated wood, and could be bought in an ironmongers shop. More often than not, they were inherited by the youngest in a family, to be put away at the end of the season. Hoops came in several sizes and were mostly taller than the children who ran along at their sides. These enormous rings were sent bowling down the road by a touch of the hand, with the owner running in hot pursuit. Up and down we would go, up and down the whole length of Britannia Road. In our family no one ever actually owned a hoop, but there was always some generous child who would let you have a turn with theirs.

Tops were not so expensive as hoops, and a penny or penny-ha'penny were within our financial range. There were different kinds of tops, of course, but, in general two types were used. One was shaped like a flat-topped mushroom with the stem tapered to a point by a metal stud. The other type was turnip-shaped, with shallow grooves running around its circumference; we called these Window Breakers. Whips could be bought; they were made out of a piece of brightly-coloured wood, with a leather thong attached to one end. But we preferred to make our own, for a good whip was half the battle. All eyes would be on the lookout for a suitable piece of string which shouldn't be too thick or too thin. The handle was not so much of a problem. Ken would whittle away with his pen-knife to transform some rough wood into a slender pliable rod. When all was ready, we set the tops spinning and then whipped them in short bursts up and down Britannia Road. I was one of the ecstatically happy children who was able to keep a top spinning for hours on end. Although our tops hopped, skipped and jumped. I never saw a window broken. Each game had its season, as did dibs (five-stones), conkers and cards. If we saw a man outside a shop who had just bought cigarettes, we would always ask, 'Can I have the card please, Mister?' These playing cards featured a famous personality, place or object. They would be placed upright against a wall. Two or more boys would then, in turn, flick other cards at them. The last player to knock the last card down won all the cards that lay on the ground. Conkers were much like the game as played today. There was the same grand talk by the owners about 'Mine's a Ninety-Niner!' Recipes for hardening winners were varied; it might be to part-bake the conker, or to soak it in paraffin, or vinegar. Ginger Blake, Ken's friend, said that his Dad recommended soaking them in the 'Po' overnight before baking. Ken confided to me that he didn't really want to win Ginger's current prize conker. Ginger's father had a great sense of humour.

IX

Christmas was a lovely time for us children. I soon got on to the bandwagon of carol-singing for money. Ken and I would go out together but not often with Dorothy as she was such a delicate child and very chesty. After each night's carol-singing, we would get home and eagerly count our takings; we got between two to three shillings on our best nights. Takings varied from night to night, however; we always did better in the poorer areas than we did in the so-called posh ones. With our takings we could buy Mum and Uncle Joe a little present and, of course, get something for each other and Dorothy. On Christmas Eve, we hung our socks on the end of the bed and no modern child with all the expensive gifts of today could have appreciated its contents more than we did. Each sock would contain an orange, an apple, some nuts and a small present. Mum paid tuppence or thruppence every week to a toy-and-bicycle shop on the corner; she always made sure that we each had some present for Christmas. Sometimes we had rabbit for Christmas dinner and once we had a chicken that Uncle Joe won in a draw. It was lovely for us to have Mum home for a whole extra day.

We didn't get much fruit when children as it was considered a luxury. We had the odd apple or orange from the free meals, as I have said, and I can remember once buying a ha'penny bag of fallers from a shop. There were few trees in Northam, let alone apple trees. The gardens, if they could be called that, were so small, only about twelve feet square. I was not above going to the Kingsland Square – an open market – early on Sunday morning to ferret around in the discarded rubbish of the previous Saturday night. Ken was much too snooty to come with me as he was now above that sort of childish thing. Sadie was not so fussy. Carefully picking over what had been left in boxes or even what was lying on the ground, we often found half a good banana or apple or orange, which we would eat with relish.

The Kingsland Square market sold just about everything. Stallholders bellowed out their prices in fierce verbal competition. One stallholder made his own sweets and toffees on the spot. We children would watch in fascination as he kept flinging the soft, sweet mixture over a suspended hook. He flung, pulled, then took the sticky substance off and then flung it on again, all-the-while his future sweets and toffees growing larger and larger. When it was to his satisfaction, he cut it into different shapes and left it to set. Old Harris, with his second-hand clothes, did a roaring trade and he never stopped talking. If a garment or shoes didn't fetch his price, he put them aside for another market day. He only sold quality goods: no rubbish from old Harris. His fast-talking held his audience and he made his customers laugh at jokes I could not understand. He was a one-man show in his own right. Business went on till late at night, lit by paraffin flare-lights. In that area of St Mary's Street, all the shops stayed open till late. Careful shoppers, who had to watch their pennies, would come late to get the last of the meat and fish for, as there were no refrigerators and the food would not keep, they would come away with bargains. I wished I had some money with me, on one occasion, when it was snowing and was cold and dark. The fish-monger sold his last lot in large mixed assortments – a carrier-bag full for only two shillings. Some lucky people must have had a bumper fish supper that weekend.

We played marvellous games of 'relievio' and 'dab' in large gangs, with the whole street taking part. Some of the young married women even joined in the skipping game. A huge rope was twirled from one side of the pavement to the other. We skipped in and out to the chant 'All in together, this frosty weather'. Our community spirit was tremendous. Once, some out-of-work theatre artistes came and did a turn in the road with a piano on wheels; for mere pennies, they sang and danced. A man in a blond wig, who was an acrobat, made a great impression on the crowd. Old and middle-aged housewives came out and joined in the acts, including my Aunt Gwen who had black laughing eyes, a large mouth and who was forever smiling. Out came two broomsticks and she danced her own version of a Scottish Sword Dance. The fact that she was the mother of a large brood did nothing to lessen her vitality. When she laughed out loud everybody knew who it was. The actors said that they only toured the poorer districts, for that was where they could get the most support.

The kindness that was the prime motive for people in opening their doors to others in greater need was not always disinterested. Although, as children, we were taken in to neighbours' houses because they took pity on us, I always felt that we were more tolerated than loved. Some wanted an errand-girl-cum-scullery-maid-cum-child-minder for their own children and, in one instance, as a companion for a doddery old lady. I was sent to one old lady when Mum was ill. The kindly doctor had sent her to the Home of Recovery, which was really meant for people who were convalescing after an operation. He somehow got her in, just to rest, for she had once again worked herself to a standstill. All Mum needed was food and a period of rest from her endless toil.

The son of the old lady had arranged for me to stay with her; it was to be for our mutual benefit. I was given a roof over my head and food while she had someone with her when her son was at work, for he was one of the lucky ones who had a job. I was eight and went to school in the ordinary way, but I was given jobs to do before I left in the morning. I got the coal in for the fire, made the beds as well as I could, and was grumbled at for not emptying her chamber pot. It made me feel sick to do this. The old lady insisted on me drinking up any sour milk that was left over, for it would do me good she said and would be a pity to waste it. I was also given the task of going to the back toilet with her. She was very shaky on her feet, her hands were like claws with black finger-nails and her face incredibly lined. The combinations which she wore had three buttons at the back, which I had to undo and then do up for her. The cheeks of her buttocks hung down in folds of flesh. This nauseating performance made me late on more than one morning for school, and teacher showed her disapproval by rapping me across the knuckles.

The old lady had a huge, black, iron kettle, which balanced on a trivet attached to the open fire, and once when I was taking it off, the heat of the handle was too much for the kettle-holder – the kettle was too heavy for me anyway – and I dropped it. I got a badly scalded leg and foot which kept me away from school, which by the way, was not Northam school. When the School-Board Attendance officer made inquiries, he notified Mum who had only that very day returned from the Home of Recovery. She asked

Uncle Joe to come and collect me and so I was rescued from the old lady, with whom I had been for six weeks – it had seemed more like six years to me. I was back in my own home with Mum, Ken and Dorothy. Things were back to normal.

X

Old 'misery' Meecham lived on the corner of our road, and we did our best to make him live up to his name. He had a garden hedge which was the object of constant attacks by us. Standing well back from it, we would form a queue and then take a running jump into 'misery's' hedge, which was prickly and rough but which stood up to our combined weight rather well. It did, however, lean inwards and we were able to lie on it and bounce up-and-down, which was quite as much fun as going to the Fair. We nearly died of laughter when 'Fatty' Harding hurled himself at it and, unfortunately picking on a thin section of the hedge, went straight through to the other side. Sometimes 'misery' Meecham would creep out and throw a bucket of water over us. Once, I remember, he decided to attack us from the rear. The crafty old man must have been waiting for us in the next garden with his bucket of slops. Four of us children were facing his hedge, and he caught us from behind. His 'favours' were spread pretty evenly over the four.

Such a flagrant affront demanded retaliation. One of the bigger boys – 'Ginger' – came up with a lovely plan. He would take Meecham's gate off and leave it in the next road. We waited until the coast was clear and crept back to take his gate, which wasn't as easy as we had first imagined, as the pivot-thing was rusty and made an awful noise. Ginger wasn't perturbed but raced off to get some of his mother's dripping. He returned with a knob of the stuff and forced the grease into the offending places. He very gently eased the gate to-and-fro and, when he thought it was well enough greased, another boy helped him to lift it clear of the pivots. The boys carried the gate to Rochester Street, the next street, and it took a couple of days for it to find its way back to 'misery's'. We now had a new and exciting game. In due course 'misery's' gate travelled far-and-wide. He even tried tying it on with rope but a sharp knife soon put paid to that. If people passed a spare gate leaning up against a wall, their only thought would be 'I must remember to tell Mr Meecham where his gate is.' The fun couldn't last forever and when we were finally threatened with the police and a good hiding from our parents, it was time to stop. None of us children had a hedge of our own and most of us had front doors that opened on to the pavement. Old Meecham had no children of his own and, if we were any example, I expect he was glad he didn't!

Once, when Mum was away in hospital, and Ken and myself were considered old enough to look after ourselves, Dorothy had a fight with one of the children from down the road. She came flying to our door and hid behind me. In hot pursuit came a big, red-faced, and very angry woman. I looked up at this towering, raging creature and wondered what on earth I could do to protect Dorothy; my legs were beginning to feel distinctly on the wobbly side. The red-faced woman waved her finger and shouted a tirade of abuse at us three children. The upshot of it all seemed to be that my wicked sister had hit 'red-faced's' dear little boy – who was bigger than Dorothy – and that we could thank our lucky stars that Mum was away. If Mum hadn't been, 'red-faced' wouldn't have been able to answer for what might have happened. She stormed off, after giving the front door a great bang. Phew, I didn't want any more of that if it could be helped! Dorothy stayed in for a while, and then I let her out to play. When I went to check on her, I found the self-same wicked girl playing quite happily with her former victim. As I passed, the red-faced mother avoided my eye. I knew, and so did she, that she should have apologized for bursting into Mum's house. 'She's only a kid, and she'll soon forget about it,' was what she probably thought; but I always remembered. Whenever I ran an errand for her, I made sure that she had the most burnt loaf, the boniest piece of meat, and the most miserable-looking vegetables I could find. Mum had never liked her – she was such a malicious gossip – and she often crossed over the road to avoid her. Mum had neither the time nor the inclination for associating with her sort. 'If you can't say anything good, then don't say anything bad,' was her comment on such people.

One morning, when I called for Pat to go to school, her Mum told me: 'Pat's not going today, tell teacher she's got a cold, will you. You can come in and see her if you like.' I saw Pat, who looked all right to me. 'You lucky thing,' I said. 'Mum wouldn't let me stay home for a cold!' 'I haven't got a cold,' she whispered. 'Mum has taken my shoes to the pawn shop, to make up the rent money.

They are nearly new and she couldn't think of anything else to hock.' 'It's the Bevios treat the day after tomorrow, you must have your shoes for that,' I whispered back. This was an annual treat for poor children in the town area; it included a charabanc ride and a tea party. Pat at once became crestfallen but the school bell was ringing so I had to go. On the way to school I wondered if Pat would get her shoes back in time for the treat. For the time being, there was no point in calling for her to play, as she couldn't come out barefoot. When the day of the treat arrived, Pat, all smiles, turned up – with her shoes. I ran up to her and said how pleased I was that she could come. 'We didn't half have a job,' Pat said. She had made a lot of fuss about it not being fair, and her Mum had pleaded 'For God's sake be quiet and shut up, or your father will hear you. He doesn't know about Hollis's,' (which was the name of the pawn-shop). Her mother promised to get Pat's shoes back if only she would stop making such a fuss. The way Pat's mother got round it was to put her wedding ring in hock so as to raise the money for the shoes. As a replacement 'wedding ring' she bought a brass ring from Woolworth's. Pat swore me to secrecy and, after that, whenever I saw Pat's mother, I used to wonder whether the ring was gold or merely glitter. Pat's mother had a great weakness for horses and she often had rows with her husband about betting, or so Pat assured me, but I rather think that Pat was a little inclined that way herself. She was always saying, 'I bet you a halfpenny, or, I'll toss you for it.' I was perhaps like Mum in believing that 'A bird in the hand is worth two in the bush'. We never went to the pawn shop.

When Aunty Flo had kittens or puppies she didn't want, she would do her best to find good homes for them. If she wasn't able to, we all knew what would happen to them. The man down the street drowned them. I was there once when he came and took the soft little pups away from their mother who, this time, had had far too large a litter. He put them in a sack and carried them out to the back yard. He filled a big bath with water and picked up the wriggling sack from which muffled yelps could be heard. This horrible man then put the sack in the bath and held it down until all struggle had finished and no more bubbles came up to the surface. He looked at me: 'There's no need to be upset, it was all over in a minute. I've probably saved them a lot of grief, in the long run.' This man also used to dock a puppy's tail, by biting it off with his nasty, yellow teeth. When I told my friend Pat, she said: 'That's nothing, our Gran always puts the kittens that she can't give away down the lavatory pan, before their eyes are open, and flushes them away, one at a time.' I didn't know the word 'callous' then, but that was what I felt it to be. I couldn't imagine Mum allowing such a cruel thing to happen. When I was older the R.S.P.C.A. opened a branch on the town side of Northam Railway Bridge and there should have been no more need for such cruel practices. I used to look at the horrible pictures of ill-treated animals in the window and would wonder how people could be so cruel. It was here that we took our cat Trixy when he became too old. The lady attendant took him from me very gently: 'He will go to sleep, my dear, and he won't wake up. I promise you that it will not hurt him.' At least some grown-ups understood the tenderness of children.

Another side of animals and their effect on us in Northam is shown by the following incident. One day, Uncle Joe came in and said to me: 'Quick, Nance, there's some dung in the road, Go and get it for me, there's a good girl.' I rushed to get a bucket and shovel. We would never miss a chance to collect manure for our small garden. As I approached the hot steaming pile, Sadie was hurrying with a similar purpose from the opposite direction. It was no good saying 'I saw it first.' So, being diplomatic, we decided to take half each. There was rather a lot; it must have been a very big horse. We divided it in half and put our share in our buckets. Just one perfectly-rounded dollop remained. Sadie, very generously, said to me, 'You can have that one.' Not to be out-done, I replied, 'That's not fair – we will have half each.' I chopped it in half with my shovel, and so justice was done.

XI

Something very odd was going on in our house between Mum and Uncle Joe. I couldn't put my finger on what it was, but I knew that they had been having words. It was all so unusual. As I entered the room they stopped talking but not before I heard Mum say: 'Well, at least you might be civil to him.' I wondered who the 'Him' could be. The puzzle was ended when Uncle Joe told me that we were going to have a new lodger; a childhood sweetheart of Mum's who

had been born in Chapel and went to the same school as Mum.
'Apparently,' Uncle Joe confided, 'now your Dad is dead, he's
courting your Mum again.' The childhood sweetheart we learned
to call 'Uncle Jim' became our new lodger. He was married but
lived apart from his wife and wasn't able to marry Mum as his wife
was a Catholic and so wouldn't divorce him. Uncle Jim was tall and
handsome; fair-haired with dimples in his cheeks and a smiling
mouth which revealed straight, white, even teeth. His eyes were as
bright a blue as Uncle Joe's but had the added allure of thick,
dark, curly, long lashes. He had travelled all over the world for, as
Uncle Joe said, 'Uncle Jim' had an itchy foot and couldn't stay in
one place for long. With his ready wit and his charming smile, the
new lodger could have charmed a bee off a flower; he didn't,
however, charm my Uncle Joe.

Mum positively glowed in the presence of Uncle Jim and she
seemed to take on a new bloom. He was on the dole but Mum was
still working. What a difference, though, once he was living with
us, when Mum came home from her charwomen's jobs Uncle Jim
would have the house cleaned and a meal waiting for her: 'You sit
down, darling,' he would say, 'I'll wash up for you.' To us three
children he was a delightful man, who would hold us spell-bound
with his stories of far-off places. We played cards and ludo with
him and he taught us 'round-the-clock' patience. Nothing seemed
to be too much bother for this paragon of virtue. He would stand
on his hands on two upturned half-pint glasses, his feet nearly
touching the ceiling, or balance on one hand on the edge of the
table with his body held horizontally. He juggled and enthralled us
with his sleight-of-hand feats; there was always some charming,
diverting, and enthralling trick which Uncle Jim had up his sleeve.
At this time, Uncle Joe almost took a back-seat. 'He's no good,' he
would tell Mum, but Mum was happy and trusting and remained
deaf to his warnings. Uncle Joe's manner towards Uncle Jim
became distinctly cool; there was even some talk of his leaving.

Because I was tall, grown-ups readily expected me to act and
think like a much older child, and because we were very close and
there was no one else to whom he could unburden, Uncle Joe
confided in me. I was only ten; perhaps he shouldn't have spoken
to me in the way he did about Uncle Jim, but Uncle Joe was trying
to make me see through him – even if Mum couldn't. The prospect
of Uncle Joe leaving home was deeply disturbing to me. 'Please

don't go, Uncle,' I would plead. 'You mark my words, Nance,' was his bitter reply, 'he's all mouth-and-trousers. He's shallow and irresponsible. Your mother will rue the day that she let him over her doorstep.' Uncle Joe didn't leave us, Mum seemed to be happy, and Uncle Jim carried on being his usual, charming self – until Mum told him that she was pregnant. His answer was just to disappear. No note, no excuse, just an over-night flit. Once again, an unkind fate had rained its blows on Mum. It was just as well that Uncle Joe hadn't left us, for Mum had to rely on him very much in the coming months.

I often thought of Mum over the years as being like a line of dazzling white washing, at which some malevolent spirit would throw mud. She just straightened her shoulders, lifted her head up, and looked her neighbours in the eye – asking sympathy from no one. 'I've made my bed, and now I'll have to lie on it,' was all she said. She picked up the tatty threads of her life and just carried on working. She was so thin that the small bump in her front didn't attract attention if she wore a loose-fitting coat, so she was able to work right up to the day she started her labour. Mum asked her employer if she could have the week off, and he agreed. She couldn't afford to lose her job – there were few enough of them – and somebody else would have been only too willing to take hers. Within a week of her new baby, John, being born, Mum was back at work. John was a gorgeous-looking baby, like one of those cherubs in a religious picture. Once again, it was Aunty Flo who came to the rescue: she looked after John while Mum was at work, in fact, until he was old enough to go to school. Uncle Joe doted on him, and I always associate John's years as a toddler with him standing on Uncle Joe's feet and the two of them shuffling around the room chanting: 'Waddle like a duck until your feet get stuck.' It was their favourite game and John never tired of it. He was a happy child and we all adored him.

For Saturday dinner, Mum would sometimes get fish-and-chips: sixpenny-worth of chips and two pieces of fish, half a piece of fish for her and Ken and half a piece for Dorothy and myself. This was only when she had enough money, however, otherwise it was just a penny bag of chips each for dinner. Once as I waited with Mum for what we appreciated as a treat, fat, know-all Mrs Cook from across the road was in the fish shop. She watched Mum ordering fish and

chips: 'You don't want to give them fish, my dear, it won't do
them any harm to just have the potatoes,' she advised. I had
already heard *her* asking for 'four plaice and two bobs-worth of
chips.' Plaice, mind you, not common cod, and I remembered that
there were only three adults living in her house. I wished I had the
courage to tell her to mind her own business, the nosey old bitch.
I knew that her family never went without anything, for I sometimes ran errands for her. But children knew their places then, and
Mum would not have thanked me for being rude I just had to keep
my feelings to myself.

The same woman was one of my worst customers, sometimes
saying that she would pay me next week as she didn't have any
change with her. I always had to remind her, and her inevitable
reply was :'Are you sure? I thought I paid you.' I was equally sure
that she damned-well knew that she hadn't. Some of my regular
customers were dears and some were devils. A Mrs Fry used to
give me a penny and a rock-cake, which did its best to defy my
healthy young teeth; I swear she used cement instead of flour.
Some of them would say, 'Come in,' and opened the door wide,
while others transacted their business through a crack in the door,
as if the transaction was something to do with the Secret Service
and they didn't want to be recognized.

We abused the chairs so much as children that the rungs were
forever coming out and Uncle Joe was, as constantly, mending
them: 'Why on earth can't you sit on them like normal children?'
he would sigh. On one occasion we must have been treating them
even more roughly than usual because he had only recently repaired
them, yet one chair was again requiring his attention. He seemed
unusually cross about it but he got on with his glueing job, and put
the chair in another room, out of the way, to set. The next day he
proudly brought the chair to us and said: 'Now, you little blighters,
see if you can break that, it's as firm as a rock.' He then plonked
himself down on it, and the leg fell off. Even Uncle thought it was
funny.

He was a Jack-of-all trades but master of none. He used to let me
help him decorate a room, and it was rather like a scene from a
Charlie Chaplin film. First, I would be sent to the Ironmonger's
for twopenny-worth of whitening which was like lumps of powdery
chalk. I would get it home and put it in a bucket and crush it to a

powder, then a squeeze from the blue bag and enough water to make a smooth paste would be added. When Uncle Joe was ready and he had got up on the box in order to reach the ceiling, I would hand the whitening to him. I usually wore his old Alpine and Ken's old shirt. Uncle took the bucket from me and wobbled on his improvised steps. I then got the lot over my head; it was obviously going to be one of those days. I removed my new-style hat and, after mopping-up operations and a change of clothes, I once more went out for another twopenny-worth of whitening. We wouldn't have any further mishaps with this new lot. Uncle Joe would let me cut the borders of the wallpaper for him, as it was cheaper than having it trimmed in the shop. The wallpaper was always thin because it was the cheapest variety and the paste was made from ordinary flour. After getting a couple of pieces on the wall, Uncle would turn to me to say, 'Well, how do you like that, Nance?' As he spoke, the strip left the wall and fell over his head and shoulders. If a piece of wallpaper was put on upside down, it would have to stay in that position as it would tear too much if we tried to put it on the proper way up. The last strip to go on by the door was sabotaged by Dorothy rushing in and through the wallpaper which he was holding up and perkily asking, 'Do you want me to help you, Uncle?' As becomes a good man, Uncle Joe could always laugh at himself.

Another job with which I always assisted Uncle Joe was mending the fuse in our dark, narrow hall. I had to hold the torch and shine it up on the fuse-box for Uncle Joe, who stood on his makeshift box and could only just reach the fuse-box. One night, as I was helping him, he was laying down the law about the dangers of electricity. 'You must always be sure that the mains are off first, Nance,' he said as he did something to the fuse box. There was a flash and a popping noise, and Uncle Joe fell off his perch. 'That's funny,' he grinned as he picked himself up, 'I could have sworn that I put the mains off first'.

His attempts at plumbing were equally chaotic. Putting a new washer on a tap was, for him, a major operation. Likewise, for years we had an old piece of rag tied around the fractured pipe under the sink to catch the drips after undoing the screw on the waste pipe because the water wouldn't run away, he must have crossed the threads in putting it back, as well as fracturing the lead on the U-bend, now if we forget to put the bucket back, there would be a wet pool on the floor and it was always damp there. Yet, as Uncle Joe was so kind and willing at all times to help Mum, she never had the heart to say 'Leave it alone, Joe,' but would simply say: 'That man's got a heart of gold. I don't know what we'd do without him.'

It cost tuppence at the barbers to get the children's hair cut, so when Mum was finding it hard to scrape up sixpence for the three of us, Uncle Joe offered to save her the money by cutting our hair. Mum diplomatically refused his kind offer, especially as Ken was heard to mutter under his breath, 'He's not cutting mine, I'm going out.' Once, I had a free permanent wave at a ladies' hair-dressers: the apprentices used to practise on 'volunteers'. Four of us girls went, and for a short while, my wiry, unruly hair seemed to be tidy. I was one of the lucky ones as my friend's hair went all frizzy, and her mother was so angry that she went to the shop and had a row with its owner. She was given the dusty answer: 'Everybody has to learn, Madam, and nobody forced your daughter to come.'

Mum worked from six to nine in the mornings, and from four till eight or nine in the evenings so we did not see as much of her as we would have liked. We used to love Sundays when she was at home all day. The only nice thing about having lodgers was that it meant that the house wasn't empty when we came home from school. Because Mum was undernourished, she was in hospital with pneumonia when Mr Green, the lodger who followed 'Uncle Jim,' made his presence felt. He had one room in the front but, as he appeared to be fond of children and was rather a friendly sort, he often came and sat in the living room with the family. One day, I was indoors with my cousin Kath, and Dorothy; Mr Green was there as well. He gave the other two girls sixpence to go to buy some sweets; sixpence was a lot of money then. When I started to go with them, he pulled me back: 'Here is sixpence for yourself. You stay here with me!' Dorothy and Kath were off like a shot. He made me sit beside him on the sofa and started to stroke my arms and body. I was eleven and, although I did not know or understand what he was doing, I was afraid without knowing quite why. I managed to disentangle myself from him and ran into the garden, but Mr Green followed. I jumped over the low wall and ran into the empty house next door the back door of which was open. He jumped after me, and followed me into the house where he caught me in the kitchen and pushed me against the wall. He pressed hard against me, and it seemed as if he had an iron bar inside his trousers. His eyes were hot-looking; they were brown with yellow flecks in them, and I could see the hairs in his nostrils and in his ears. His face was prickly, his lips were wet, and there was a sort of dribble running down his chin. Looking up over his shoulder, I could see a red-plush picture frame left by the previous owner. Queen Victoria gazed regally down at me from inside the frame. Mr Green kept pushing hard against me; his hairy hands were hot and shaky, he was making queer, moaning noises, and was breathing very heavily and sweating. I don't know where I got my strength from, as my legs felt like jelly, but I made one last desperate effort and pushed him away. I fled, fear lending wings to my legs. I ran straight through our house and out into the road, where I found Kath and Dorothy who had returned from the sweet-shop. Kath was two years older than I, and I incoherently stammered out: 'Don't go in there, Mr Green has been horrible to me!' It took a few minutes for her to get any sense out from me, then she left me outside with Dorothy and rushed off to tell her mother. In no time at all, Aunty Flo came back with her, and a few moments later Uncle Joe appeared as from nowhere. I was interrogated by both of them as to what had actually happened. They kept on at me: 'Tell Aunty what he did'. 'Did he do anything else?'. 'Did he hurt you?'. On and on Aunty and Uncle went. I had had a very lucky escape. I was very frightened for I knew that Mr Green had meant me harm, without being able to understand just what harm he had intended. Uncle Joe was white with anger; his usual jolly face was quite unrecognizable. He told us to remain where we were and went into the house, leaving the front door open. We could hear raised voices, scufflings; and the sound of furniture being moved about. Then there was quiet. Suddenly, Mr Green came hurtling out of our front door and his belongings, which were fairly sparse, followed. He seemed dishevelled and agitated. He hurriedly picked up his belongings and almost ran away up the road.

We then returned to the living room where two chairs lay on their sides and the table was skewed in the middle of the room. When Uncle pushed the table back against the wall, where it usually lived, he found a sixpence on the floor. I was puzzled to see him lift the round lid to the top of the stove and drop the money in the fire. He answered my questioning glance by saying in a quiet voice: 'It's dirty money, Nance.' We didn't have any lodgers for some time after Mr Green's departure.

XII

Northam really went to town in celebrating the Coronation of George the Sixth in 1937. In Guildford Street we had a tremendous party, with everybody's kitchen tables and chairs in a long line down the middle of the road. The houses were festooned with flags and bunting and we all wore red, white and blue, even if only in the form of a ribbon. Hats were home-made and came in all shapes and sizes. Everybody going to the party took something for the tables, which were groaning with jellies, custards, fruit, cakes and sand-wiches. The school children brought their own blue coronation glasses, which had been presented at school. When the tables and chairs had been cleared away, some of the adults had their own glasses and they weren't drinking lemonade! We Northamites danced and sang to accordions, banjoes, and even a piano which someone had got out on the pavement. Best bib-and-tucker was worn, and old ladies frizzed-up their hair for the occasion. One little old lady did a clog dance in her husband's great boots, and we danced the Veleta in long lines up the street. Others found 'Knees up Mother Brown' as entertaining, and there was much exposing of bloomers. Grown-ups joined in with children at games like 'The big ship sails through the Alley Alley Oh' or 'Ring a Ring of Roses'. One man did several recitations, some of which drew shouts of laughter from the grown-ups; Uncle Joe did the Sailor's Hornpipe and then everybody joined in with 'Nelly Dean'. Many small heads were nodding when 'Auld Lang Syne' and 'God Save our Gracious King' had been reached. It was indeed a grand and memorable day. The old enjoyed it as much as the young, who went to bed tired but happy. It was our own King and Queen; they belonged to us as much as we belonged to them. We were British and proud of it.

When I was twelve, Mum was ill once again with pleurisy, and she had to go into hospital. Mrs Thomas from across the road kindly offered to take me. Ken could look after himself, and Dorothy went to Aunty Bell's. Mrs Thomas was young and pretty. Her husband was the same age and worked on a boat. They had a five-year-old daughter, Mary. I was company at night for Mrs Thomas when her husband was at sea, and useful as a nursemaid for Mary. The food was excellent. Mrs Thomas loved cooking and her husband used to bring home plenty of food when he returned from a voyage. I saw a whole ham cooked for the first time there. She was kindness personified, and even bought me for Christmas a dress at C & A's. Little Mary was a delightful child. I did, of course, help Mrs Thomas but it was more of a pleasure for she used to work with me and we chatted together in such a friendly way. During my stay I was desperate to see Mum, but how was I to get to the Southampton Chest Hospital? Then I remembered the Alans. At her front door in Graham Street, Mrs Alan sold toffee apples for a halfpenny each and, if you went up the Cut, in Clarence Street, you would come to Mr Alan's back garden from which he hired out bicycles at a penny an hour. Mrs Thomas gave me the money and I hurried to Mr. Alan's. I'd never seen so many bikes together; he had them to fit any size of person and there must have been at least twenty. I told him that I wanted one for two hours and gave him the tuppence. He sized me up with a glance and nodded towards one of the bikes: 'That here is about your size.' He was perfectly accurate in his assessment. He warned me about over-staying my two hours. 'It'll cost you another copper if you're late back'. This was my first real bike-ride but I put my foot on the pedal and scooted down Mr Alan's path as if hiring a bike was for me an every-day occurrence. I had been given clear instructions as to the way and, within half-an-hour of leaving Northam, found myself being admitted to Mum's ward.

All the other visitors were carrying flowers or fruit, and I felt naked as I entered for I had nothing. I looked for Mum but didn't at first recognize her. She was the white-faced woman three beds up from the door. She called to me. Her dark hair was loose and spilled out upon the pillow; there were now a few silver-hairs in it. I looked at Mum's two hands which lay resting on top of the folded sheet; they were white with the blue veins clearly defined. I hadn't until then, realized that she had such well-shaped hands; they were smooth and soft and white. Gone were the chaps looking like knife-cuts, and the callouses. Everything about Mum looked pale and even her eyes seemed faded; she hardly looked like Mum. I kissed her on the cheek, and spoke the usual clichés like 'How are you?' but it wasn't what I really wanted to say. We talked as people will of unimportant things, not being able to express the love and anxiety we both felt. 'Is the cat alright? Is the brass on the front-door still shining? Are you being a good girl? It was very kind of Mrs Thomas to have you.' Etc. The hour seemed to go both slowly and quickly. At last the bell sounded and it was time to go. I left thinking how small Mum had looked in her hospital bed, and asked God to 'Please make my Mum well again.' I arrived back at Mr Alan's in good time.

Mrs Thomas had five married sisters, each with children. Occasionally, they all went out with their husbands to the pub and left me with their little dears, eight or ten of them, I seem to remember, at one time. The youngest was very young indeed, and I earnestly prayed that he wouldn't wake up and cry; fortunately, he never did. The other little dears I did my best with but, as children will, they quarrelled and if, under extreme provocation, I smacked one, I would hear a chorus of 'I'll tell my Mum when she gets back.' The smaller ones would gradually fall asleep in chairs, and I would carry them upstairs to bed. Mary wasn't any trouble and I liked her as much as she liked me, regarding her as a younger sister. Some afternoons the sisters would gather at Mrs Thomas's for a cup of tea. On one such afternoon, I was in the garden putting some washing through a large but old mangle, which has wooden rollers, when I mangled one of the little one's fingers. With so many children underfoot, I had not seen her put her hand onto the washing as it went through the mangle. Her mother was very cross with me, but after some brief tears, the child calmed down; no bones had been broken. I felt really shaken and very guilty.

Towards the end of my stay with Mrs Thomas, I once again got into trouble. She and her husband had gone to the pub and left me with Mary, who was asleep upstairs. I felt bored and thought that no-one would see me if I took Mr Thomas's new bike out for a ride. I wasn't worried about Mary as she never woke up after she had been put to bed. I was already feeling rather disgruntled as I had won an Art Scholarship at school, and should have been attending classes after school at the Art College in New Road. I was not allowed to go for I had to attend to Mary. Also, I now didn't have the time for doing any odd jobs which would bring in pocket money. You can now realize why I felt fed-up. I went into the shed where Mr Thomas' new bike was kept. I rode up and down the road several times on it; it was smashing. It should be remembered that not many men in our road owned a bike. I decided to go further afield. At the end of Radcliffe Road was the level-crossing and, on the other side, some shops and a pub. I was riding by the pub when who should appear but Mr Thomas. I stopped dead in front of him. To say that he was angry would be an understatement. I had used his bike without permission and, worse, I had left Mary unattended at home. I was really in the dog house. The two Thomas' had a row and I had to go back home. I was told that 'I was an ungrateful girl, who was old enough to know better. I didn't know when I was well off . . .'.

I was only too pleased to go home for Mum had been out of hospital for several weeks. I soon had my errand jobs back and was earning pocket money once more. My Art Teacher was angry with me for not taking up the Scholarship; it was too late, I was told and I wouldn't have another chance. I didn't feel like explaining why I had not been able to attend the classes; there seemed little point. All of us children could draw, I suppose it was a family trait. We even used to quarrel about whose turn it was to have the paper for tracing from inside a packet of tea. As I was sitting at the table drawing an angel, Ken, back from work, was drawing ships. He had a lovely new rubber, which was black at one end and white at the other. 'Gosh, where did you get that!' I demanded. With the superior air of the older brother, he replied, 'Pinched it!' and snatched it back. He had not really pinched it but was only being awkward. I kept on thinking about the rubber and then told my friend Sadie about it. We decided to go to a large store and steal one.

On the counter, next to the rubbers was a section with celluloid dolls some five inches high with a pink and blue feather stuck on the head to represent an Indian head-dress. I stole one of those as well for Dorothy. I felt like a real criminal when we got back to our street and stood at the top worrying about where we could put our loot. Suddenly, I knew that I didn't want to take it into the house. What would I say if I was asked, 'Where did you get that doll? And where did you get that rubber?' I persuaded Sadie to take the doll and rubber to her bedroom. I went home guilt-laden. Her mother sent for me that evening. Sadie, my *friend*, had told her mother! Her mother told me that a private detective had been watching me, and that it was only due to the fact that I was without a father, and that Mum had been ill, that he did not report me. I was given a lecture and told that I would not be allowed to so much as speak to Sadie again if I ever repeated such a terrible act. Her mother then put the doll and the rubber on the fire. I was glad to see them burn. Although the detective was imaginery, I had been so badly frightened that I didn't disbelieve her and, wonderful woman, she didn't tell Mum. I spent a rotten following day and night, but the incident gradually faded from my memory and I then felt really forgiven.

While I was living with Mr and Mrs Thomas, Mum let two rooms to a father and son. They had the middle room downstairs and the middle room upstairs. The son was a cut above the usual type of working man, having good regular features and every hair on his head was kept firmly in its place. He always looked as if he had just come back from having a short back and sides at the barbers. His father was very old and fragile-looking, with parchment-like skin. The son looked after his father with great care and tenderness. Their two rooms were spotless; the windows shone, and the fire-place gleamed with a rich blackness. There was never a speck of dust to be seen. They were both as scrupulously clean with regard to the clothes that they wore. A heavy, brass-bound Bible took pride-of-place on the table. Once a week, the cupboard containing their food was opened in our presence. The father would give each of us one oatmeal biscuit taken from the biscuit-tin on the shelf, replacing the tin in precisely the same position. The son was punctilious when addressing Mum or us children. He knocked very politely before coming through our living room to get to the kitchen so as not to inconvenience us, especially at meal-times. Mum had never had such perfect lodgers before, and they were so quiet! It was difficult to know whether they were in or out. Mum would tell us that they were almost too good to be true.

When the old man died, Mum kept the curtains in the front pulled as a token of respect. The son continued to lodge with us and Mum was grateful for having such a considerate tenant. If only she could have seen ahead. Perhaps, however, it was just as well that she couldn't.

XIII

During all these years of growing up Ken had treated Dorothy and myself with the disdain usually shown to lesser beings. He did the things that boys usually do: cutting his fingers with his Scout's knife; falling out of trees or off walls, and coming home to quote Mum, as 'Black as the Ace of Spades'. Ken always managed a splendid selection of bruises, bumps, and perpetually-skinned knees which we could admire. He was always the one in charge of the fireworks on bonfire night – although we had to do our stint with the guy on Northam Bridge. He did the buying of the fireworks because we didn't know which ones were best, and he would only let us handle the sparklers. When our prying fingers clutched at the pretty-coloured tubes in his box, they were swiftly deterred by a shove or slap from him. 'It's too dangerous for children,' Ken would say, sounding for all the world as if he were a hundred-and-one years of age. Ken forever had the bottom out of his trousers and Mum would say, as she sewed on yet another patch: 'I don't know how you do it. You should have been born with feet on your behind.' Time and again, he had to be sent back again to wash his neck as his first effort usually produced a tide-mark. 'It's a wonder you don't block the drains,' Mum would sigh at him. When Ken was reaching school-leaving age, his trousers were again a problem. He couldn't go to work in short trousers. The situation was resolved by a Provident check, and as he earned, so he would have to pay it off. A check was issued by a private finance company to be exchanged for goods in specified shops. A deposit of 5% was put down and the balance called for by an agent over the next twenty weeks. Mum didn't like checks, although they were in common use round about, because the things were worn out before they were paid for, she always maintained. Just for this once, she had to bow to the inevitable as to pay cash for them was out of the question. Her son was going to look as good as the others, but we were warned not to let on about the check to others.

Ken was now fourteen and had started work in a shoe-shop. Every little helped, and he was good to Mum. He even gave Dorothy, John and myself a few pennies. Uncle Joe bought a wireless from Curry's for some money down and then an instalment of sixpence a week. Our excitement was truly electric! Mum had a pink glow to her cheeks and we children were getting under Uncle's feet. He unwrapped the shiny black-and-white set, and shushed us up while he read the instructions. You could have heard the proverbial pin drop. One end of the sideboard was cleared and the wireless was placed on it as reverently as if it had been the Crown Jewels. There was a great length of wire called an aerial, and I failed to understand why it was called a wireless at all, if it had to have all that wire! I kept badgering Uncle for an explanation and he got cross with me. We all filed out to the garden, to watch Ken shin up Mum's washing-line pole – he swayed about a bit whilst doing his stuff – which added to our excitement. Then we all rushed indoors again as Uncle connected up. 'Hey Presto!'. Music came out. I made a cover for the wireless from an old dressing gown, and it was religiously covered up when not in use, at least until its novelty wore off. Only Mum and Uncle Joe were allowed to touch it. We were, indeed, entering the electric age.

Now that Uncle Joe was working he was able to give Mum a little more money, and he sometimes had kippers for his tea. I used to watch his plate in case he left any skin or bits, and I knocked them back pretty smartly if he did. I would also go to Snell's in Northam Road to get a quarter of corned beef for his sandwiches. Snell's was a cooked-meat shop, with a workman's café at the back. Although I had gone there on errands for other people, I had not, until then, gone for Mum. Apart from corned beef and all manner of coloured sausagemeat, there was always a whole leg of ham and a whole leg of pork on dishes in Snell's. Two great platters would contain dripping, of both pork and beef, which had been turned out upside down to reveal the thick layer of brown jelly on top. Mr Snell was like an artist the way he would sharpen his long, slim knife with a steel which hung from his waist. He would cut delicate slices of his meat and flip them with considerable dexterity on to greaseproof paper. I was so puffed up with pride that I felt like telling him: 'It's for my Uncle. My Mum is going to put it in his sandwiches. He's got a job and he's working again'.

It was at this time that we nearly had a chicken for dinner. Mum had been ill again and the kindly butcher had asked a neighbour of ours if she would deliver a bird for him to our address; he also sent Mum his regards, and wished her a speedy recovery. We didn't know anything of this, until I had to go some few days later to the butcher's for Mum. He asked: 'How is your mother now? Did you all enjoy the chicken?' Puzzled, but not wishing to appear ignorant, I replied, 'She's much better now, thank you, and the chicken was lovely.' I could hardly wait to get home and tell Mum of our strange conversation. Mum fathomed it out in the end. Mrs Smith who was asked to deliver the bird had a large, hungry family; she was very hard pressed for money and had failed to resist the temptation of our chicken. 'The poor woman must have been desperate to have done such a thing; no wonder she's been avoiding me', was how Mum put it. She could feel compassion for Mrs Smith who had put her own family first. 'What a cheek', I retorted. 'Surely you'll say something to her.' Mum smiled: 'You're too young to understand, Nance,' she said. 'Mrs Smith has got more troubles than I can possibly explain to you. Of course, I'll have a word with her, but I can't be angry with her.' It didn't seem much of a temptation to me, and I said so. 'When you're older, I'll tell you,' Mum sighed. 'As I've often said, Nance, you can always see someone worse off than yourself.'

As Uncle Joe was in more regular work as a rough painter in the docks and things were now a little easier for Mum, he bought some chicks and built a coop in the garden for them. The sweet, little yellow balls of fluff lived in the warm living room until they were old enough to stand the cold outside. If it was extra-cold, they would be brought in, even when they had grown to a fair size, and kept in boxes in the kitchen. Uncle Joe looked after them as if they were his babies. They were to provide our own Christmas dinner and be presents for some of my Auntys and Uncles. I used to worry about the smallest of the bunch, a poor little thing, who looked so thin and scraggly with its skin showing through the featherless places. The others were always pecking at it, and guzzling most of the food. My heart went out to this waif. I pleaded with Uncle to take it out and build it a little box of its own. 'It won't make any difference, Nance,' Uncle told me. 'They are just like people. You get them at the top that grab everything and them at the bottom who get the dregs of life. All the others, in between, are like the in between people like you and me. If I take that poor, skinny thing out, we'll end up having two poor skinny things, because the other birds will pick on the next weakest.' I felt an affinity with that lowly unfortunate chick.

The big dark, strutting cock was like the father of one of my friends who was always crowing about what a fine fellow he was. The largest, high-breasted hen seemed to me to resemble a woman up the road who was forever standing at her front gate and tearing some unfortunate's reputation to shreds. This woman had beady eyes and a beak-like nose; her head would jerk up-and-down as her thin lips swiftly did their dirty work and for a second or so after each sentence her mouth would remain fixed in a screwed-up position. Yes, there could be no doubt that she looked like our largest hen, for she even folded her arms high on her ample bosom. Uncle Joe managed to get in a bit of his political indoctrination with the chickens when he told me that 'The have-alls at top, like the cock, were Conservatives, and the have-nots at the bottom, were Labour.' I'm afraid that I would have been a great disappointment to my Uncle in my later years.

It was Ken who introduced me to smoking. He was fourteen and I was twelve. He let me try a cigarette, one of a packet of five Woodbines. I felt sick afterwards but, naturally, I didn't tell him. Ken was so proud of my achievement as a smoker that he brought his friend in to watch me at it: I made a good job of it, just like a film-star. Selecting, in a casual manner, a cigarette from the packet – looking as if I had done it many times before – I held the cigarette in the elegant manner between my nail-bitten fingers. Leaning back in the hard upright kitchen chair, I drew on the fag after Ken's friend had lit it, and forced the smoke down through my nostrils. I thought I did this really well; so sophisticated, I felt. By the time that I had finished the cigarette my eyes were full of water and my stomach felt as if tied up in knots. I didn't feel much like the film star of the short time before and I staggered drunkenly to tne toilet, while Ken and his friend roared with laughter. I well remember this occasion because Ken had said, 'Never mind, Nance here is something for your Spanish refugees,' and he gave me a sixpence.

That same day, I had come home from school full of what the teacher had told us. She said that a train would be coming in to Southampton station packed with children from Spain, mostly orphans, or children who had been separated from their parents when fleeing from Franco. Many of the children did not even know whether their parents were alive. Would we ask our mothers, teacher urged, if they could spare a little something for these children as they might not have eaten for some time? The School Authorities had arranged for us children to go on to the platform and hand our gifts through the train windows. We were asked for sandwiches, biscuits, cakes, and if possible, a few sweets. We didn't, of course, understand about Franco, but the plight of these children tugged at our hearts. Mum didn't let me down and from somewhere came up with three paper-bags filled with food. The following day, large numbers of we luckier English children poured on to the platform with our small offerings. In addition to Mum's bags of food, I carried twelve halfpenny bags of sweets which I had bought with Ken's sixpence. The train was already in the station and was packed tight with children of all ages. We were astonished to see that most of them were semi-bald, and their dark eyes looked enormous in their naked heads; they had recently been deloused. We Southampton children eagerly reached up to the windows along the whole length of the train and the excited Spanish children clutched our remarkable assortment of bags, all the while gabbling away in their, to us, incomprehensible language. Mum's three bags and half of the sweets disappeared through one compartment window and the rest of the sweets through the next. Some of the Spanish children looked bewildered, and some of them seemed to have been crying, but many of them were smiling and I knew that they were saying 'thank you, thank you' in their own language. The train did not stay for long and, as it moved off, we all waved furiously to each other until it had gone out of sight. I was deeply moved by what I had seen and I felt more than grateful that I had Mum and Uncle Joe. When I told them about it that night, and especially about their semi-shaven heads which seemed to me so cruel, Uncle tried to explain how necessary it was to crop their heads. Fleas, he said, were carriers of plague and it was better to be safe than sorry. Mum's comment was: 'It's better to have no hair, than no breath, it'll soon grow again.' The next day our teachers thanked us all and said that they were very proud of what we had given, but I knew that what I had given was really due to Mum. For several days, I couldn't get the thought of the Spanish children out of my mind, and I wondered where they had gone, and if they ever found their parents again. My musings, as is the way of children, were not of long duration and I soon got on with my own life.

At the time that the Germans were invading Poland in September 1939, we listened in complete silence to the wireless news bulletins at home; to interrupt was more than we children dared. Uncle Joe and Mum discussed these events but what they said was above my head. I couldn't make out Uncle's change of opinion. I could remember him previously, telling me what a remarkable man Hitler was: 'We could do with somebody like that over here, he pulled Germany right out of the mud.' Uncle Joe had been to Europe when a young man and had told me that the Germans were a hard-working race and very clean. He had also told me, as far as being a housewife was concerned, that the first place was taken by the Dutch women and the second by the Germans; and that he wouldn't have minded one for himself. Now all that had changed: instead of calling them 'Germans', he called them 'Huns' or 'Jerries' in a nasty kind of voice, they were Barbarians. Mum said, 'Thank God for that' when Neville Chamberlain returned from Munich, waving his piece of paper, and telling the British people that there would be peace in our time. Uncle Joe agreed, though he later told me that we should have called Hitler's bluff over Poland. 'At one time,' he would wistfully say, 'we would only have had to threaten them with a gunboat.' There was now much talk between Mum and Uncle about digging a trench in the garden. Some people, Uncle asserted, had already done so. I can remember him saying, perhaps in order to calm us, 'But we'll wait and see, it might blow over yet.'

The last year of my school life was now drawing to its close and I was to go to the Summer School for a fortnight's Camp. I had always wanted to go but there had been no money. Now, however, Ken was working and Mum decided that she could afford the ten-shilling charge. That was only half the battle for, besides money, I was given a long list of clothes to take which we didn't have, such as two pairs of underdrawers and a pair of overboots – I didn't even know what they were! We Northam children never wore white cotton underdrawers under our navy-blue knickers. However, that was the least important item. The mac and cardigan that I didn't possess were the most worrying. These, I managed to borrow. I had my one-and-only pair of shoes to take the place of the overboots, solid walking shoes, plimsolls and slippers – all of which we were told were absolute essentials. Children would not be allowed to take more than ten shillings spending money for the fortnight. I went off with my hard-earned 1/10d and was very pleased with myself. It was June 1939 but I was oblivious to the world situation. However, its seriousness was becoming increasingly apparent. On our third day in Camp, all of us girls were assembled and told that the King and Queen would like us to do some very important work for them. We were taken to some huts in coaches and there confronted with strange grey-and-black rubber objects with round filter discs. We had to put a rubber-band round the disc to attach it to the mask-piece. They were called gas-masks. Our camp was at Lee-on-Solent, and we had only once gone down to the beach. The rest of that week we continued with our war effort and at the week-end we were told that our holiday would have to finish, and we would all be returning home. So much for my eagerly anticipated holiday! Instead of teaching us about how one-fifth of the world was red and British, we should have been taught something about Hitler, Mussolini and their kind.

We children who went to Stubbington Camp, as it was called, were accompanied by Miss Goodman, our Art teacher. I idolised her; she was so beautiful, and so kind to me. She allowed me to take home paper and paints whenever I liked. It was kindred-spirit stuff, I suppose; I was always very lucky in that way. Every time I looked at her I was put in mind of the head of a Greek goddess in a cameo. Her natural, platinum-blonde hair she wore on the top of her head in an enormous bun; her wide-set, large, bluey-grey eyes were spanned by lofty brows, her nose was Grecian and, when she smiled, she showed her even white teeth. My Greek Goddess, however, had one flaw – she was bandy! As we were all about thirteen to fourteen years of age, and she was young, we could talk together on easy terms. At the Camp, we all badgered her to let her hair down: 'Just once, please Miss!' And she did. She came into our chalet as we were preparing for bed. A gasp of wonder escaped from us all in the room as Miss Goodman entered our chalet in a full-length satin night-dress of clinging lavender, with her glorious hair cascading in soft waves to the top of her hidden legs. Never before, or since, have I seen such a gorgeous woman. Our cries of 'Oh, Miss, you are lovely,' brought a blush to her cheeks. She wished us goodnight and returned to her room at the end of the chalet. I thought to myself that God had truly compensated her lower half by making her top-half so extraordinarily beautiful. Miss Goodman was my last teacher at School and she, like me, was leaving but, in her case, to get married. I could only get tuppence for the collection for her wedding present. Some of the more affluent girls brought a shilling and I was almost ashamed to put such a small amount in to my favourite teacher's collection. I felt even worse when she discreetly gave me a drawing book on my last day. In 1941, Miss Goodman, my friendly Goddess, was to become a prisoner-of-war of the Japanese in a crueller kind of camp.

It was at Stubbington that I asked to see the nurse, who was an elderly, soft-spoken Scotswoman. I had felt two cracks appear behind my ears. She examined me and told me, 'My child, you have eczema coming. You will have if off and on all your life. You will never lose it entirely.' She was, unfortunately, right.

I was to leave school in July and I was looking forward tremendously to this. I thought that I was already very grown-up for, in the gang of girls that I had taken up with, we did our usual larking-about with boys. One night, one of the big boys kissed me, he was a baker's apprentice of fourteen, fresh from school. He forced his tongue between my lips; I was so ignorant that I thought I would have a baby. I found that I could always talk to Mum so I told her what had happened. She managed to reassure me. Another boy I went out for a walk with one evening was Ken's best friend, so I felt quite safe with him. I was wrong. He, too, had left school and was fifteen. He was very handsome, or so I thought, and I was flattered by his attentions. I was still a very tall, skinny girl, but strong and wiry. We took a long walk over to Bitterne, laughing and chatting all the way. I was having a good time. He put his arm round me and I felt very grown-up. Just like a courting couple, I thought we were. We walked by a row of half-built houses and stopped by one which had its front door open. 'Let's have a look inside, shall we?' Ken's friend suggested. 'Yes, all right,' I said, and in we went.

With a suddenness that was truly amazing, the Handsome Hyde, turned into a Horrible Jekyll. He seemed to have an extra pair of hands. Without any preamble, his hands were under my coat and skirt, attempting to pull down my navy-blue knickers. He got them down nearly to my knees. As I tried to get away, I found myself shackled by my knickers and overbalancing, we both fell down. It was fortunate for me that I was as strong as I was, for a weaker girl would not have stood a chance. I fought with everything I had. I bit him, pulled his hair, kicked, and struggled to the limit of my strength. After what seemed an unending period, we were both exhausted, and the breath sobbed in my lungs. I crawled away from him, and as I got to my feet pulled my knickers up at the same time. I was out of that door in a flash.

He hurried behind me, very red in the face, and begged me not to say anything to Ken. He had a large scratch across his nose and his eyes were watering. I, myself, must have looked as if I had been drawn through a hedge backwards. He hung back all the way home, attempting to placate me, saying how sorry he was: don't tell your brother; give me another chance; he didn't know what came over him; and always it was please don't tell Ken. It eventually occurred to me he was scared of what Ken might do to him. By the time we got to the top of my road, I had recovered my composure. I still had not spoken a word and left him a picture of abject misery. I did not tell Mum or Ken. I don't know why I didn't, but I just didn't.

It was decided by the employment officers, who were supposed to fit school-leavers into appropriate jobs, that I was fit only for domestic service. I was to start work the first Monday after leaving school in a large Private School, on the outskirts of town, as a house parlour-maid, living in and earning six shillings a week. Some charitable organization paid for my two blue cotton morning-dresses, full white pinafores, two black grosgrain afternoon dresses with four frilled organdie aprons and caps to match, two pairs of black wool stockings, and a pair of black shoes. So there I was, on the verge of adulthood and ready to face the wide world. My childhood was at an end.

PART TWO

WIDE WORLD

XIV

On the outbreak of war, Uncle Joe had to move the chickens to make room for an air-raid shelter in our tiny garden. He loved his garden and allotment and took a delight in growing things. Each year, runner beans climbed up a rope along the same wall, making a long, dancing curtain of green leaves and red flowers; tiny pink roses climbed over an arch just outside the back door. If anyone had green fingers it was my Uncle Joe. When he and Ken dug the shelter, they dug deep and, on the earth covering of the shelter, Uncle grew marrows and tomatoes as splendid as any that I've tasted since. Like everyone else, Mum had already parted with her front railings and gate. She added every bit of copper, brass, steel-fenders and saucepans that she could lay her hands on. The men who came to collect the metal asked for gold if at all possible. Mum's only gold possession was her wedding ring. I wouldn't have been at all surprised if she had handed that over as well. She was an easy touch for any man at her door, especially if he had a hard luck story to tell.

She had once bought, for ten shillings, at knockdown prices, a roll of useless lino. The fast-talking salesman had told her that it was his last roll and, as he was in a hurry to get back to his sick wife, he was letting it go 'cheap'. Mum parted with her ten bob, a lot of money then, and found when she unrolled it that the pattern was only along the outside edge; it split and tore at the least excuse. Another man at the door said that he would enlarge, frame, and colour a snapshot for her for a very reasonable price and wanted a five-bob deposit. Mum kept waiting for him to return but would always say: 'He was such a nice man. Perhaps he's not been very well.' Gypsies frequently plied their wares at our door. I remember that the women wore a shawl tied round their necks to hold a baby on one side, while on the other they would carry a large basket of pegs, flowers, and bunches of lucky heather. Mum always bought her pegs from them but couldn't afford the flowers. Once, thinking that a gypsy baby looked blue with cold, Mum gave its mother a small wool blanket, asking the gypsy to return it on her next visit. 'Bless you, my dear, have a bunch of heather, you've got a lucky face,' the gypsy woman replied, but Mum never saw the blanket again. Mum was so soft-hearted and trusting that she was the despair of all her sisters. Aunt Bell used to say of her that 'She would give her arse away, and shit through her ribs if need be'. Although the expression might be somewhat coarse, it was a very apt one for Mum who gave to others, without stint, all her life.

It was a Sunday afternoon that I first set out as a working girl. I carried my new uniform in a paper parcel and caught a tram as far as it would go, and then had a rather long walk until I reached the school. I walked up a long drive hemmed in by tall trees, which took me to the front entrance of a magnificent house. I nervously rang the door-bell which was opened by a grey-haired lady. I managed to stammer out that I was Nancy, the new maid. 'Come in,' she said, 'I have been expecting you, but you must never use this entrance again. Servants use the back door at the rear.' The hall had a dark oak parquet-floor and grand, wide stairs, which branched in two about halfway up. I had never seen such grandeur before – except on the films.

First of all, I was given my detailed instructions. I was to address all adults in the school as Sir or Madam, except Cook, whom I was to call Cook. I was to get up at five-thirty in the morning and, in my morning uniform, make tea. I was to take tea to the lady and her husband in bedroom number one. 'At the moment,' she told me, 'we have only two teachers in residence, the others are on holiday and will not be back for two weeks.' Having dealt with the tea, I was then to clean the front porch and polish the brass on the door and, after all that, clean the hall and stairs. I would have time, she assured me, to polish the dining room and sitting room before serving breakfast in the dining room at eight o'clock sharp. I would have my breakfast afterwards in the kitchen with Cook and the scullery maid. I was to wash the glasses and silver in the pantry; the plates and dishes in the scullery would be washed by the scullery maid. I was to clean and dust in the bedroom and the school rooms, not at that moment in use for the children were away on holiday. Then I was to wash and change into my afternoon uniform. Lunch was served at noon, light tea at four o'clock, and dinner at seven o'clock. On no account was I to use a rough cloth on the surface of the dining table; any bits were to be swept off with the crumb-brush and tray. The grey-haired lady was sure that I would like it and that I would soon settle down. She showed me all over the house and, when we reached the topmost attic rooms, told me that I was to share one of them with the scullery maid. I was then taken downstairs to meet Cook and Carla, the scullery maid. Before we entered the kitchen she told me 'Your wages will be five shillings a week, and your half-day is Wednesday. This Wednesday, just to start with, you had better stay and clean the silver.'

We entered the kitchen. Cook appeared, all dark and greasy, like the kitchen itself, the walls of which were festooned with large pots and pans. Carla was a tiny black-haired beauty with olive skin and enormous liquid eyes. She was fourteen and had arrived only an hour before me. Carla spoke only broken English, having not been long in England. Her family had fled from Spain when the Spanish Civil War had ended. It was her first job. Our birthdays were on exactly the same day. Cook had shown her what to do. We were both told to go to our room and get changed into our uniforms.

As we went up the narrow, uncarpeted stairs at the back of the house, I asked what her name was. She replied 'Carla'. I told her that my name was Nancy. The small room we were to share had two, narrow iron beds and a chest of drawers. On the door there were two hooks for our coats and some nails in the wall, just in case we might have any other clothes to hang up. We looked into each other's eyes and confessed that we were not going to like it here. After putting our pitifully few possessions in the chest of drawers and changing into our uniform, we returned downstairs.

I was shown how to lay the table for tea; to serve on the left and to take away from the right. After tea, I was told to clean the pantry as it had not been cleaned for some time. This would occupy me until I was shown how to lay the table for dinner. I remember that on the sideboard there was a melon on a silver dish, bigger than a football, which had to be placed in the centre of the table. When dinner was over and I had cleaned the pantry, probably the first thorough cleaning that it had had, we 'dined' in the kitchen where Carla had been helping Cook. We went to bed at nine o'clock as we were told that we needed our sleep if we were to get up fresh in the morning. We both lay in our beds talking far into the night. The strangeness of the place, the tall whispering trees outside, the scary hooting of an owl, and the sense of being cut off from our homes and families, formed a bond between us. We must, eventually, have fallen asleep for I was woken by the shrill ringing of an alarm clock at my bedside. The grey-haired lady must have put it there during the night. It was five-thirty. We both quickly dressed, washed, and started on our duties. Carla had to take a cup of tea to Cook before she raked and made up the boiler, etc. That whole week, including our supposed half-day (which Carla spent cleaning out the kitchen cupboard) rolled by in non-stop days of work. I was told to clean windows in any spare time that I might have. We had to sit in the kitchen each night after dinner, ready to cut sandwiches or make tea or cocoa should the Masters or our employer feel at all peckish later. It was usually around ten-thirty or eleven o'clock before we were eventually free to fall into our beds.

Each night, Carla talked of ghosts; her family were some sort of spiritualists. My hair would literally stand on end at some of her stories. We both had desperate longings for home. On Sunday afternoon we were paid our first week's wages, and were told that, although the grey-haired lady was satisfied with us, we were rather slow, and would have to work in earnest when the new term began and the other Masters returned, and that some forty children would be waiting to be served at lunch-time. Carla and I looked at each other; we both had the same thought – we would run away.

When we went to bed, we prepared for our moonlight flit. Carla had brought her clothes in a case but I had lost my brown wrapping paper and was in a bit of a fix. I tied the sleeves of my blue morning dress tight around the waist and stuffed the skirt-part of it with my few possessions. My five-bob wages I clutched in my hand. Our part of the house was very quiet, so I thought now is the time to flit. Carla wasn't so certain and thought that we should wait a little longer. 'I'm going now,' I said, and that was the last I ever saw of her. I crept down the back-stairs, with my heart in my mouth at every creaking the stairs made. With my bundle held tightly under my arm, I slipped past the kitchen, from where I could hear voices, and reached the servant's entrance door. It was for me the week-old

Maid's EXIT door. Once through I had the long driveway in front
of me. I walked on its grassy edge as much as I could because, in
the stillness, the pebbles of the drive made such a noise. I was
waiting for one of Carla's ghosts to float at any moment from the
trees. At last, I reached the pavement outside and breathed sighs
of relief. I didn't want to break into my two whole half-crowns by
getting a tram ticket; I wasn't sure, in any case, if they would be
running so late. So I walked home.

It was a dark night but warm, and my heart and my feet seemed
light. I was going home to Mum and Uncle Joe, Ken, Dorothy and
my little brother John. How I had missed them all! When I
reached old, familiar Northam Bridge and then our road, I wondered
what I would say to Mum. I opened our door and went through
into the living room. Mum was there on her own and about to go
to bed. She looked at me in amazement. 'Whatever has happened!'
she cried. I burst into tears and told her that I had run away. Mum
put her arms around me and listened while I, between tears, told
her of the misery of the past week. 'You silly girl,' Mum said, 'you
don't know what hard work is.' 'But I do know, and nothing will
make me go back again,' I replied. Mum took my bundle, which I
had been still holding, and I gave her my money, still hot from my
hand. She made me a cup of tea and told me to go to bed. Mum
wrote a letter to the grey-haired lady and went out to post it that
same night – it was very probably past midnight. The post was a
lot quicker in 1939 so, within two days, Mum received an answer,
demanding the return of the five-bob and pointing out how ungrateful a girl I had been. Mum did not return the money. We
afterwards noticed that the same school were always advertising
for servants in the *Echo* the local evening paper.

When Ken was sixteen he left his job in the shoe-shop and went to
sea in the Merchant Navy. For a long time he didn't tell Mum that
he had been present at the evacuation of the Channel Islands, in
case she would be worried. Soon after war had been declared the
small boat on which Ken worked was one of the armada of rescue-
ships sent to the aid of the Islanders. He told me that the boats
were loaded to capacity with frantic Islanders trying to get out
before the Germans came, and that the dockside was piled high
with merchandise from houses and hotels. People bargained goods
and valuables with the ships' captains in order to obtain a passage

to England. The lucky ones found standing room only on the boats, and all their precious possessions remained on the quayside. As soon as he could, Ken joined the Royal Navy. Uncle Joe would have liked to have joined up as well, but he was too old. He had been a sailor during the great Influenza epidemic of 1919, and loved to tell us of his experiences. Apparently, his whole ship's company had gone down with 'flu except, of course, Uncle Joe and the ship's doctor. They kept going for three days and nights on rum, nursing the 'flu victims, until totally exhausted they collapsed on the deck. Uncle assured us that the ship's Doctor thought that he, Uncle Joe, should have been made an Admiral at least!

It was Uncle who organized the war effort in our home. He would put his gas-mask and Warden's helmet on the sideboard just inside the door, so it was forever falling at our feet. After it had fallen on Mum's toes, she complained: 'That helmet's getting more dents on it in here than its likely to from Hitler's bombs outside.' It continued to occupy the same precarious position till the war was over. Buckets of sand and water were at the ready in case of fire, and we had three dustbin lids by the back door, to put over our heads as protection when running for the shelter; a sort of metal umbrella in case it rained shrapnel. Uncle Joe didn't think much of my jokes, when imitating a Chinese wearing my dust-bin hat, I would lisp: 'Me lun velly clickly, makee legs lun fast'. Uncle would grunt back: 'You'll laugh on the other side of your face, my girl, if they drop one on the gasometer!'

XV

I had only been unemployed for a day when Sadie knocked to say that she had spoken to her employers about me, as she knew that they needed another maid. Sadie was two months older than me and worked at Mayes in the High Street. I went immediately to apply for the job and was taken on the spot, to start the next day. The wages were six-bob a week and I was to live in. So I was to earn a shilling more than I did as parlour-maid at the school. Mayes was the grandest emporium in Southampton. Super-drapers and undertakers; as Undertakers, they were open day and night. The shop-front was graced by a doorman who, when it rained, would escort customers with a huge umbrella, from their cars to the shop entrance. Mayes was many-storied, and at the top lived all the people thought necessary to run such an establishment. Some of the buyers lived in, as did some of the departmental managers. The young girl assistants and lesser fry, who did not live in, had a dining room which was the size of a small hall. We servants had our own sitting room next to the big kitchen.

I was one of four girls who served lunch at four long tables. The vinegary cook produced meals reminiscent of herself: small portions which were not very appetizing. We all knew when Molly, the other cook was on duty, for the vinegary cook kept down the cost of everything to impress Madam. Her books would show how little she spent on food. Molly, on the other hand, didn't care a damn about that. She had a gorgeous laugh that came right up from her belly, and her meals were generous to a fault. She treated everybody alike: 'Come and have some more, ducks,' Molly would say, 'there is plenty here.' Madam liked Molly. She spent more time in the kitchen when Molly was there. Molly made her laugh as well. The two cooks worked alternate shifts – six o'clock until two, and two o'clock until ten. The vinegary cook and Molly did not live in; Gladys, their assistant, did. She was a shrivelled old maid, who had dirty personal habits. She would poke the dinners about with her fingers, which had often been up her nose or thrust in her ears. One day, seeing her do this, and feeling greatly daring, I said: 'Don't do that, Gladys, it's dirty!' She cackled back: 'What the eye don't see the heart don't grieve over, dearie!'

I helped all over the place, cleaning the maids' rooms and washing up in the kitchens, which had double sinks and draining-boards made of wood. The wooden draining-boards became soft and slimy after use, so I furiously scrubbed and rinsed them so as to leave them looking nice. At night, when it was quiet, the cockroaches came out to roam about at will over the sinks. We couldn't help the cockroaches! Mayes was kept beautifully clean, as I was made aware when serving in the buyers' dining room.

I shared a bedroom with Sadie and another girl. If the work was hard I didn't notice it, as I was very happy there. We had many laughs in our room, and could look down from our great height at the High Street below. We used to think that we could see 'Jersey Lil' there. The other girl told us that she was a bad woman who did rude things for money. Her mother had told her, and both Sadie and myself were round-eyed at this information.

The lady called Madam was a strange woman. She picked up my empty handbag one evening and put a half-a-crown in it. Her maid told me, so I thanked Madam, but she was rather cross with her maid for telling me about it. I couldn't help noticing Madam's eyes, the pupils of which sometimes seemed enormous. She was rather old, and wore a red wig and had many lines on her heavily made-up face. A monocle hung from a chain around her neck. Madam walked with a silver-topped, black stick. She was a drug addict, or so everyone said, which might have accounted for her up-and-down moods. I was always treated well by her.

The first time I helped wait on the buyers, I managed the soup and dinner well enough, but when I was hurrying along with a large silver tureen of rice I tripped and upset half the contents on the floor before reaching the Dining Room door. I scooped the rice up with my hands and flung it, little bits of dirt and all, on to the tureen. I rushed back to the kitchen and grabbed two cloths, one of which I used to wipe around the edges of the tureen, and the other to wipe my hands. I entered with the third course, placed it on the table and collected the buyers' used plates, which I then wheeled out on a trolley. Quick as a flash I was off to the kitchen, and then rushed back, with four floor cloths, all nice and damp, to hastily remove the traces of my accident. There might have been a few sploshes left on the wall but nobody would have noticed it on those walls. When I returned with the coffee and started to clear the tureen and plates from the table, the head buyer asked me to, 'Thank cook for the lovely dinner. The nutmeg in the rice was simply perfect!'

I started going out with Sadie at nights. We were allowed out after we had served tea, but had to be in by ten o'clock. I even had time to go home if I wished, which made life a lot sweeter. I noticed that Mum and Bob the lodger were becoming very friendly. He would go out for a pint of beer, which was his limit, and bring back a Guinness for Mum. He became friendlier each time I came home, and showed his affection for Mum in many small, attentive ways.

Sadie and I would flirt and joke with boys when we went out together, and we enjoyed the feeling of growing-up. We put lipstick on and, at night, rolled our hair in pipe-cleaners, costing a penny ha'penny for twelve from a tobacconist's. As they became more difficult to find, we used bits of electrical wire. Sadie and I did our humble best to look glamorous. One boy who took me to the pictures twice, bought me my first real present! A case for my gas-mask which had hitherto remained in its cardboard box, slung over my shoulder by a piece of string. People were supposed to carry them at all times.

Sadie had changed almost out of recognition. The chubby, round-faced, very saucy child had become a slim, self-assured young woman of five-foot nothing. Her straight, thick, jet-black hair was arranged in waves and curls, and her lively blue eyes were fringed with soot-black lashes. She had always had black lashes which now seemed to be an extra adornment. Sadie would never need to wear mascara. We were complete opposites as regards both temperament and physique. Sadie was as flat as a board in front, and she was so conscious of her flat-chestedness that she used to stuff cotton-wool into her bra. She didn't need a bra really. it was only of use to hold the cotton-wool padding. Sadie was always saying: 'I wish mine were as big as yours, Nance.' She could have had my bust any day; I would willingly have exchanged it for half of Sadie's wit. Everything seemed a joke to her, and boys hung around her like bees around a honey-pot.

It was during my time at Mayes that I was told to go downstairs and see two children who were asking for me. I remember that it was a bright, sunny September morning. I ran down the many flights of concrete steps at the back and found Dorothy waiting with John my little brother. Dorothy was twelve and John just four. 'We are going to be evacuated,' Dorothy told me, 'we are going on a train to the country.' 'I'm going on a puffer,' John announced. 'Mum said that we had to come and say goodbye to you,' Dorothy said. 'Is Mum going with you?' I asked. 'No, it's only for children, and we can't stay long as we have to get back to school by eleven o'clock. Coaches are taking us to the station.' On hearing this, I hurried upstairs and borrowed two florins from Molly. I gave Dorothy and John one each and kissed and cuddled them. I felt disconsolate as Dorothy walked away hand-in-hand with John; the sun shone on his hair, which gleamed a light gold.

I later learnt that the train took them to Poole in Dorset and that John thought it a great treat going on a train. They had, until then, been things that shunted and whistled and thundered by at the back of our house. From Poole, the evacuees were sorted out and put into buses which took them to a large hall or warehouse, where they were given sandwiches. There was another bus-ride and a long walk to a church and, once more, the inevitable sorting out. Each time they stopped, children were taken away and so their numbers diminished. On again went Dorothy and John until they reached a small chapel where they lay to rest on the pews. The chapel grew colder; it was starting to rain and was now quite dark and John had fallen asleep. A lady saw them, and her heart went out to the tired small girl holding a sleeping little boy in her arms. They both had tickets giving their names, addresses and schools. 'Poor little man,' the kind lady said to Dorothy. 'Let's take him home to bed.' It was late by the time that their day's ordeal was over. Dorothy posted her card which she had been given to say that they had arrived safely and the next day she wrote Mum a letter. Mum cried a little when she read about John asking for her that first night, but she cheered up when she read that the people were wonderfully kind, and that John had settled in. The house had a garden as big as a field, and Dorothy thought that they would be very happy there. Dorothy still writes to them today.

Sadie and I were both mad about dancing. Jitterbugging was the thing to do at the beginning of the War. It cost one and sixpence to go to the Banister dance hall on Saturday nights. This was quite a large part of our earnings, but it was worth every penny of it as we had so much fun there. One particular Saturday night, as Sadie and I were dancing together (girls often danced together), Gil Hume, who was the dance band leader, called for silence. He asked if there was a girl called Campbell in the hall; if so, would she please go to the main door as there was an urgent message for her. I hurried from the dance floor with Sadie to find out what had happened. A policeman met us at the door. Very gently, he told Sadie that her stepfather had broken his back in an accident at the docks; apparently a crane had dropped its load on him. He was in hospital, Sadie was told, but there was no hope. Sadie's mother was already at his bedside. The police would take Sadie in their car and she asked me to go with her.

When we arrived at the hospital, I was allowed into the ward with the mother and daughter. Sadie's stepfather looked ashen-faced and his eyes were sunken. His wife, who was a Catholic, had sent for a Priest, as she did not want her husband to die before he had embraced her faith. Sadie's stepfather had been a good, kind man for as long as I had known him. He had never been a church-goer and was, so I understood, an agnostic. Sadie's mother explained all this to the Priest. The dying man was mumbling in his delirium as the Priest bent over him. 'Repeat after me' the Priest instructed him. And then followed what seemed to me to be a disgusting sort of farce. The Priest rapidly spoke in tones which seemed hardly audible. It appeared that the groans and moans of the dying man were taken by the Priest as answers. With one last gasp, Sadie's stepfather died. Her mother sobbed with joy at the thought that her husband had, at last, been received into the Catholic Church. She thanked the Priest with tears running down her cheeks. She flung her arms around Sadie, saying she was quite certain that her father had always wanted to be a Catholic. At my tender age of fourteen I was appalled and, almost then and there, became an atheist. That experience was a turning point in my life.

Sadie, naturally, was upset, but he was her stepfather, and they had had many rows in the past. The last time that I had seen him alive was the previous night. Sadie and I had gone to a dance and I was to sleep at her house. I had gone indoors while she was still outside with a boy. Mr Campbell was angrily pacing up and down in the room. The clock showed after midnight. At last, Sadie quietly opened the back door and crept in, shoes in hand, but her stepfather grabbed her by the back of the neck, pushed her through the kitchen and living room and flung her out of the front door. As a parting shot, he slipped off his boots and flung them after her. Sadie, in retaliation, flung her shoes back at him. I knew that he was only trying to be a responsible parent so, when he had stomped up the stairs to bed, I let her know that the coast was clear and we both went up to bed. After his death, she said she wished that she had been more considerate to him as he wasn't a bad old stick. She was, however, more concerned at her mother's anguish.

Sadie couldn't stay subdued for very long, and her natural gaiety was well in evidence within a fortnight when we were off dancing again. As we were chatting after that dance, Sadie told me how she and the boy she was with had a strange experience. He had placed one hand very cautiously on her left breast and, encountering no resistance from her, had become bolder. While caressing her breast, he had dislodged the pad of cotton wool and had followed the bump down until it reached her waist; at this point, he took his

hand away in utter bewilderment. Both of them simply pretended
that it had never happened. Sadie went through the whole pantomine
with graphic gestures, and we were both convulsed with laughter.

XVI

By this time we had barrage balloons, shaped rather like a small
Zeppelin without the gondola, cluttering the sky. The steel cables
to which they were attached were supposed to deter low-flying
German aircraft. German fighters sometimes shot them down; I
once saw four shot down in as many minutes. They were mostly
silver in colour, and glistened prettily in the sun. Air-raid Wardens
paraded the streets at night to enforce the black-out regulations,
ensuring that no lights from windows or other places could be
spotted from German planes. We didn't have any thick curtains, so
Uncle Joe got hold of a dark brown blanket as a makeshift and
hooked it over our living-room window, using the two nails on each
topside of the frame. In Bob the lodger's room, he made a sort of
roller-blind from thick black paper, for Bob was hopeless at any
form of improvisation. The kitchen window was only about
two-feet six by eighteen inches, so that presented little problem.
The other rooms he dealt with one at a time, but we usually went
to bed in the dark. We had always to remember to put the light off
at night, before opening the door to the outside. Many people hung
a curtain of black-out material some three feet back from their
front doors to prevent a light showing when the door was opened.
Visitors were usually inspected by the light of a dimmed torch, for
the door was opened to a total darkness outside. During the more
frequent and serious air-raids, people often risked a fat lip by
lighting a cigarette after the siren had gone, for some people
wrongly thought that a lighted cigarette could be seen from the air,
so 'put that cigarette out' was a frequent and angry cry. Buses
were allowed only the most miserable and dim lights and they had
to stop and put out all their lights whenever the alert was sounded
at night. The vehicles that used the roads during the war, and there
weren't many of them, had side-lamps which gave about a shillings-
worth, in terms of size, of light. Headlights of frosted glass had a
metal mask of approximately three to four inches by half an inch
with three slots in them to cover them, and the former beautiful
chromium bumpers were now painted white.

Whenever I went home to see Mum, Bob would walk part of the way back with me. Once, he told me that he was very fond of Mum, and he gave me a cigarette to keep me company through the darkness of the streets.

When people heard planes overhead, they would say: 'That's a Jerry,' or 'It's one of ours.' It was pretty unpleasant when one of ours turned out to be one of theirs, as sometimes happened. Notwithstanding the war, Sadie and I were still enjoying ourselves at work and in the evenings with our boy-friends. A perennial problem for me was either that the boys were too short, or that I was too tall. We usually went out together two or three times in the week, but would mostly just stand around and have a lark. I would read books when I stayed in. I had always been a bookworm. Mum used to say in her most despairing voice: 'Its no good talking to her when she's got a book, she's as deaf as a post.' I often used to lock myself in the lavatory to have a quiet read, only to have someone bang on the door shouting: 'Come on out Nance, I know its you in there with your blasted book again!' Life seemed good for us fourteen-year-olds.

When I arrived home one evening and was going through to the living room, the door of Bob's room opened and Mum called to me, 'Come in here Nance.' I entered Bob's room, which was as usual immaculately clean. Mum and Bob seemed flushed and rather like a couple of kids, and he had his arm around Mum's shoulders. I looked at them and said, 'I know you've got married. You don't have to tell me.' Bob said, 'I'll be good to your mother and I'll try to make up for some of the bad times she's had. You can call me "Bob" if you like.' After a few months it was obvious that Mum was going to have another baby. At this time, I was recommended for a job as house parlour-maid with a Doctor and his wife. The wages were seven-and-sixpence, which was one-and-sixpence more than I had been getting. I took the job and left Mayes.

Both the Doctor and his wife were young and Jewish. Kathleen, the cook, was a Roman Catholic and a dear. Their house was beautifully furnished, and the food was never stinted. It was one of the nicest places that I ever worked in. Even though the doctor was often called out in the middle of the night, he didn't complain, the more so if he had to deliver a baby. His wife told me that he loved delivering babies best of all and, with great pride, showed me his medals for medicine and surgery. Once, when I hurt my foot,

I wore a pair of his shoes. When I slept in, which I did sometimes, it was in their lovely guest bedroom. I once broke a real china cup and offered to pay for it from my wages. His wife only laughed and said that my wages wouldn't be enough to buy it. She bought me a real leather handbag for Christmas.

There was always a bowl of fruit on the parlour table, which was constantly refilled. I could have a bath whenever I liked. Kathleen and I had the same quality food in the parlour as the doctor and his wife had in the dining room. Once, cook dressed a whole fresh salmon for dinner, and I was enchanted to see the salmon ringed with thin slices of orange. We had chicken so often that when I went to Mum's for Christmas dinner, and we had one, it had little novelty for me. What a contrast it was to my first situation as house-parlour maid!

Whenever I went home I harped on at Mum about having a bicycle. In the end, she relented and said I could have one. It would have to be on the never-never! There was a seven-and-sixpence deposit and then a series of one-and-sixpenny weekly payments. I was so excited. At Christmas, Mum gave birth to a lovely baby girl, and she and Bob seemed to be getting along splendidly. She asked him to act as guarantor for the hire-purchase agreement for my bike. To my bitter disappointment, he refused. This was the first time I had known him to be difficult and his behaviour to show signs of eccentricity. Uncle Joe could not sign the agreement as he was not a house-owner. Mum went a few doors up to a good neighbour of ours, who signed for me without any bother at all. Now, at least, I had my very own bicycle.

My first long ride was to Romsey with Sadie and two boys. As I was gaily pedalling along by the side of a fast-running stream I turned my head to laugh at something my boy-friend had said; I should have looked where I was going. I went off the road, over the edge, and my bike and myself ended up in the stream. He fished me out and straightened my handlebars; fortunately, no other damage was done. We all laughed a great deal at my mishap. I cycled everywhere. As I was going home one night, Kathleen asked me to get her an *Echo* from a paper shop down the road. It really wasn't very far, but I was in a hurry as Sadie and I were going to a dance. I cycled a little way up the road, turned round, and told Kathleen that they had sold out. My lie spoiled my whole evening, and when I returned to the doctor's house that night, I lay awake in bed, twisting and tossing. Not being able to stand it any longer, I got up and went along to Kathleen's room. I knocked on the door and Kathleen, who was sitting up in bed, asked me to come in. I explained that I had not been to the paper-shop and I had told her a lie. She smiled and said that she had known I had lied. She wished me goodnight and 'God Bless'. I now felt much better than I had done for the whole evening.

I had to learn to answer the phone in case I was in the house on my own, so the doctor's wife arranged to phone me when she was out. My speech was rather common: most people from Northam dropped their H's when speaking so, instead of saying 'Dr Black's 'ouse, can I 'elp you?' I had to say, 'Dr Black's *H*ouse, can I *H*elp you?' With some little effort, I mastered the technique and tried somewhat harder to speak more correct English.

One night, at the Banister dance hall, which wasn't far from the doctor's house, I saw a man who lived nearby. He knew Dr and Mrs Black. I was surprised to see an older man, as it was mostly teenagers who went to that particular dance-hall. He may only have been about twenty-eight, but that's quite an age to a girl of fifteen. He came over and introduced himself. After buying me a lemonade, he asked if I was going back to the doctor's house tonight. I told him that I was going home. 'Let me take you in the car,' he insisted. 'No thank you,' I replied, 'I can walk home.' 'But, you must let me take you,' he pressed, Dr Black wouldn't like to think that I let you go home on your own on such a dark night. He would think that I was most unkind.' Much against my will, and my better judgement, I got into his car. He drove to the top of my road, stopped the car, and began to say silly things to me. I can remember that he had more arms than an octopus. It was only when I promised to meet him the following night that he let me go. His parting words were: 'Don't let me down, will you. Petrol is very difficult to get nowadays.' Needless to say I did not meet him and kept out of his way from then on. I didn't tell Mrs Black.

By September, 1940, German bombers were often flying on raids over Southampton. One of Mum's sisters was bombed out from four different places. No sooner had her family collected together the essential requirements for another home than it happened again. Lord Louis Mountbatten's home, Broadlands, took a few homeless families into the old servant's quarters; my much-bombed Aunt's

family was one of them. They stayed there for many months until
other accommodation could be found in Romsey.

On September the twenty-fourth, Mrs Black was anxiously
looking for the doctor. Lunch was ready, and as the doctor was
late, in the oven to keep warm. The loud droning of planes could
be heard; it made a threatening noise to my ears. The doctor's car
then pulled up at the side entrance. As he got out, his wife urgently
called to him because we could hear the bombs whistling down.
In one wild rush, Cook and I, and then the doctor and his wife,
scrambled down the steps of the closet, which was under the stairs,
just inside the door. There was a roaring, deafening sound and we
seemed to be rocking about in a choking cloud of blackness. Our
lungs, mouth and nostrils were filled with dust, and we could still
feel heavy bombs dropping, but the thudding sound was now
further off. The doctor's voice asked, 'Is everybody all right?' and
we answered, 'Yes.' We forced the cupboard door open and, as we
came up the steps, we could see that we were lucky to have
escaped with our lives. The side of the house was partly demolished. It looked just like a doll's house with one side missing. The
car was flattened to the ground and St Barnabas' Church opposite,
totally destroyed. There was rubble everywhere. Mrs Black looked
at the wreckage of her home, and managed a little smile. The odd
things are remembered at such times, like a demolished room with
a mantelpiece still standing, and a vase that had jumped unbroken
over the clock in the middle of the mantelpiece to stand side-by-
side with the other matching vase. which appeared not to have
moved. The vicar from next door rushed up to us and implored
her to 'Come in quickly, you good people' when what Mrs Black
wanted, as she told me afterwards, was to spend a penny. These
raids over Southampton, which began in June 1940, were to
continue until the middle of July 1944 but this was the first time
that I had been personally involved. Dr Black found a temporary
surgery but it was not long before he was called up, and I had to
find another job.

XVII

This was at Pirelli's, the cable-makers. I enjoyed my work and I
liked the free dances held at the firm's club in Lodge Road even
more. I earned fifteen-shiilings a week and was really coming up in

the money-world. Pirelli's factory was an enormous place, a vast hive of activity. I was taught to repair cables that were damaged. I was the youngest on this particular section and came in for a fair bit of teasing by the old hands but it was all in good fun. Pirelli's played a vital role in the war effort and, because of the frequent German air-raids, we often had to go to the shelters. One day, the management called us all together in the Canteen and asked if we would be willing to work through the air-raids. Being young and not very conscious of the danger, I put my hand up. There were only two other hands up in the whole canteen. I realize now that the others had wives, husbands and children, and being older, they set a greater value on life. Someone near me muttered, 'Put your hand down, you young fool,' and tried to force my arm down. I stubbornly kept it up, and one of the older women from my section told them to leave me alone. She turned to me and said: 'You keep your hand up if you want to, ducks. That's your affair, you're entitled to your own opinion.' However the meeting decided that we weren't going to work through the raids.

I became quite proficient at my work. The wire ran off a spindle through an electrical tester which marked any place in the outer covering which was not sound. This unsound place was then repaired by me. I would cut away about one-and-a-half inches at a tapered angle to the bare wire, then I would bind that with fine strips of rubber no thicker than a matchstick, which I ironed with a tiny iron shaped like a six-inch screwdriver. When the shape was to my satisfaction, that part was bound in a sort of oiled-cloth and laid in a long bath of bubbling wax. After a suitable cooking-time, during which I was carrying on the same process on other wires, the repaired wire was removed from its bath, the bandage taken off, and it was now ready for testing. Only an expert could have known if the wire had been repaired; the shape and the colour were uniform.

One night in early November, Pirelli's was bombed and the part where I worked was burned out. When I arrived at work there was rubble and confusion everywhere. Those of us who had nowhere to work were told to report to someone in the canteen, who told us that we would be loaned to the Tobacco Company until other work was found for us. We were to report to the Tobacco Factory during the morning. Sadie was working there, so I was quite happy at my transfer. I could hardly wait to tell her, and when I did, she was overjoyed. 'See if you can get in the packing section where I work,' she said. 'Don't go downstairs to the stemmary if you can help it. Upstairs in the packing its clean and we wear white overalls. In the stemmary downstairs, they wear dark brown overalls and, where they strip the leaves all day, they reek of tobacco. It's horrible.' I said that I would see what I could do. When I reported to the Tobacco Company I was in luck, for I was sent to the packing section and was issued with one thick white cotton overall with short sleeves and a square neck. This was the property of the company and had to be kept clean at all times. It meant my washing it overnight and ironing it dry if it became too grubby. I thought I would never get the hang of my new job. The girl who was showing me what to do deftly placed a white strip of cardboard over a pile of cigarettes which were rolling towards her and scooped up exactly fifty with one hand, while her other took a round tin from the rack in front of her. The fifty cigarettes, encircled by the white cardboard, entered the tin in an almost magical fashion. It wasn't a bit like that, however, when I tried it. The cigarettes kept coming on, and I either picked up too many, or not enough. When I did manage to pick up the correct number I felt rather surprised. Fortunately, my instructress was patient and stayed with me for most of the morning. I think if she hadn't, I would have been up to my ears in cigarettes. After dinner-break, she left me virtually to my own devices. I wasn't doing too badly by then. All hand-bags had to be left in the cloakroom with our clothes. The job, and the security, was very strict. We were frequently stopped and searched for cigarettes when leaving the factory.

I didn't work anywhere near Sadie, which was probably just as well, but we met each day in the canteen if it was raining, or on fine days went outside to eat our sandwiches. We generally talked about what we would wear at a dance; how we would fashion our hair; and naturally enough boys. At this time I met a young man in a sailor's uniform, a gay and chatty Londoner. We hit it off straight away, and he was my partner for three weeks running at Banisters. He was a little on the tubby side, but his cheerful disposition put that small fault in the shade. He could make me laugh at any old nonsense. The first time that he walked me home, we stopped outside the house and, after chatting for a few minutes, he said, 'I've got something to show you.' He fished about in his pocket and then put a small square envelope in my hand. 'Do you know what this is?' he asked. I felt all over the packet. There seemed to be a soft ring of some sort inside, so I suggested that it was a washer. 'No. It's not a washer,' he said. 'Well, then what is it?' 'It doesn't matter,' he replied and took it back from me to put it in his pocket. 'It's of no importance.' He pecked me on the cheek and wished me goodnight. 'I've got your address, I'll be writing to you.' Then he was gone.

Many months later I had a letter from him asking me to be his steady girlfriend. He said how much he liked me, and that he would have written sooner, but had been in Hospital. he had been wounded in the leg and hadn't written to me until he was sure that his wound would not leave him a permanent cripple. He didn't think, he wrote, that it was fair to offer a one-legged chap to a nice girl like me. I was saddened by his letter, but it was such a long time ago that we had met and I hadn't given him a thought until that letter. I wrote back, as nicely as I could, refusing his offer.

The wireless was now switched on for every news bulletin; there was no need for Uncle to shush-up anybody as we all listened intently. After the Narvik fiasco, when Neville Chamberlain resigned, a Coalition Government, under Winston Churchill, took over. Churchill was a Tory, Uncle Joe couldn't deny that, but when he spoke to us with such fighting words in his own unfor-gettable voice, Uncle would square his shoulders and rather grudgingly say: 'Well, even if he is a Conservative, he's a ruddy good Englishman first!'

I wasn't with the Tobacco Company for long as work was found for me on another section at Pirelli's. It was very boring work making belts for the machines. I started to look around for another job, but continued to take full advantage of Pirelli's Dance Club, where I met a very nice boy called Charles. He wore a neatly pressed grey suit, always had a snowy-white collar, and carried a glitteringly white hankie in his breast pocket. Charles was a little shy at first but gradually he became my regular dance partner; we danced well together as he was the same height as myself, which made, as you can imagine, a pleasant change for me. How often would I be sitting out before the band started and a young man would approach me to ask: 'May I have this dance, please?' As I got to my feet, their facial expressions would vary. I was five-feet eight-inches tall, and loved wearing high-heeled shoes so, as I drew up to my full height, some of the shorter boys had actually to look up at me. Some of them would be dismayed but put on a brave face, making such a remark as: 'Oh, er, well if you are game, I am.' Others just laughed and happily took me on to the floor. Once, a cheeky young blighter just grinned at me and said: 'I've never danced with a giraffe before!' He was a really funny little chap, and we were constant partners for the rest of that night.

Charles and I, as I have said, got on well together. He said that I was a nice girl; not at all like some of those 'port and lemon' girls, who only went out with someone for what they could get out of him. I only drank lemonade. We would talk about a whole host of subjects and put the whole world to rights several times an evening. It was a pleasure for me to be able to talk to such a well-read young man. At last, I thought, 'I've met a kindred spirit.' We spent as much time talking as dancing. I was wondering when he would see me home. Finally, one night, he did. I was only too happy to say yes. 'Where do you live?' he asked. 'Northam,' I answered. Judging by the look on his face, I might just as well have said, 'Down a sewer.' He faltered, then said, 'Oh well, I don't suppose you can help that. I never would have thought that you came from a place like that. You do surprise me, but I'd still like to see you home.' I was being patronized; I felt a fierce, protective loyalty for scruffy, battered Northam take hold of me. I looked at the condescending Charles and said, 'You needn't bother. I'll see myself home. I don't want to see you again.' He attempted to speak to me on many subsequent occasions, but our former camaraderie was cold and dead.

The next boy who began to take me home behaved himself well enough for a couple of weeks, but then started the usual 'hanky-panky'. I had to warn him about his behaviour. He turned nasty, telling me in a tight voice, 'You're nothing but a P.T.' and stalked off, not only stiff legged. I didn't know what a P.T. was, so when I got indoors I asked Mum; Uncle Joe was also in the room. Mum told me as delicately as she could what a P.T. was, adding that, 'You'll get yourself strangled one of these nights, my girl, if you keep coming in late.' Uncle Joe added the further comment: 'You'll wake up and find yourself dead one of these mornings, Nance.' I then put my hands around my neck and staggered about the room like a dying duck. A faint smile started around Mum's mouth, which quickly grew in to a huge grin. Uncle Joe gave me the helpful advice that, 'If they get too tough, Nance, bring your knees up hard between their legs, that'll soon cool them off!'

One evening, after a vigorous jitterbugging session at Banisters, I was beginning to feel quite woozey. I remembered that I had drunk six egg flips, and possibly something else! I knew that I was tipsy. My boy-friend had an amorous glint in his eye and I thought that as discretion was the better part of valour, I should get away. I made up my mind to go home – alone. An air-raid had just started and I staggered homewards quite happily. Bombs were falling, guns were firing at planes, and searchlights pierced the sky, their beams waving about as if they were tipsy too. When I got home Mum was waiting for me with the baby in her arms. 'Come down the shelter at once,' she cried. I was too tired to follow her and only wanted to sleep. I lay down on a settee in the living room, and vaguely made out among all the other noise, Mum's voice urging me to get up and come down the shelter. I was too far gone to take any notice and just wished that she would go away and leave me to sleep. Mum had to leave me where I lay. I was sixteen and very stupid. Mum gave me what I deserved the following morning. I never got drunk again. Uncle Joe also gave me a piece of his mind: he took his Warden's job very seriously and he was furious at my attitude. He shook me and shouted, 'If you want to get killed during a raid, then go outside and get killed where some poor devil won't have to risk his life digging you out of the house.'

It was shortly after this incident, when I was walking over Northam Bridge with Mum, that an elderly man said 'Hello'. 'This is Nancy,' Mum said, 'my eldest girl.' 'So you are Stiffy's girl,' was the reply. 'One of the best was Stiffy, buy anybody a drink.' The man had the purple-blue nose and jaundiced-yellow eye of the hardened boozer. That, I thought, was the other side of the coin. 'He should have spent his money on his wife and kids,' I retorted. 'While we were running around with holes in our shoes, the likes of you were drinking our shoe leather.' I really went for him. Mum pulled me away, telling me, 'You're wasting your time, he doesn't understand, men never do.' I wondered if my six egg flips had done any damage to my nose. If that was what drink could do to a nose, it was best to leave it alone. I knew that I would look at mine as soon as we returned home after that particular encounter.

One winter evening, when I came home from a dance, I met at the top of our road two young men in Royal Navy uniform. They were really only boys, and one of them reminded me of Ken – tall, straight and slim. It was a bitterly cold night and the frost had made the pavements glitter in the moonlight. They were so drunk that one of them had passed out on the ground. I hurried indoors to tell Mum. She, Uncle Joe and myself helped the two back to our house. Mum's soft heart had been touched by a certain likeness of one of them to Ken, and she and Uncle Joe put them both in Uncle's bed, who would be fire-watching and wouldn't need it. When Mum got up the following morning, she took cups of tea in to the young sailors. They had gone! There was two shillings on the mantelpiece and, hanging down outside the open window, a long, yellow icicle. Mum could only smile and say: 'Poor lads, I never thought about giving them a chamber pot.' There had been no light as the electricity had been cut off, and she had not thought of leaving them a candle. Candles were not easily obtainable and paraffin stoves and lamps that had not seen the light-of-day for years, were, at this time, gratefully dug out of sheds and cupboards.

Dorothy returned from Dorset as she was now nearly fourteen and would soon be old enough to go to work. I went down to fetch her from Dorset, where she had twice moved since first being evacuated there. The first person she had stayed with had asked Dorothy to go to her sister's and help nurse a little three-year-old child dying from cancer. Dorothy was wonderful to the child, and I knew that she could be an angel at such a time. After the child's death, its mother gave Dorothy a small diamond-and-ruby ring in acknow-ledgement of all the help that Dorothy had given. It was hardly worth-while Dorothy going back to 'Aunty's' – as she called the first lady she stayed with – it would soon be time for her to return home. The second place was a house where the woman only wanted the six shilings a week allowance for an evacuee, and to use Dorothy as a minder for her two small children when she and her husband went out every night. Dorothy could never eat chocolate spread again. She had it for breakfast, dinner and tea in that house, so she wrote to Mum asking to come home.

We chatted non-stop all the way home. I told her, with a sudden burst of generosity, that she could wear all of my clothes. It was the first time that I had seen Dorothy for two years; the last time had been when she had come up to Mayes with little John to say goodbye. The small, dark-haired, short bobbed child of twelve had become an attractive long-haired teenager. She spoke in a pleasant way, having lived in Dorset with well-spoken families. Grimy, battered Northam came as a shock to her, its noise and dirt forming such a contrast to the peace and freshness of Dorset. Dorothy, however, was happy to be home again with Mum. Little John was fine where he was and, anyway, he could barely remember Northam. It was rather funny about me letting Dorothy wear my clothes for, when she opened the largest of her two suitcases in the bedroom, it appeared to be tight-packed with nice dresses, and other articles of clothing, all made by her first hostess, who was a fine needle-woman and had looked after Dorothy so splendidly. It ended up by my wearing Dorothy's clothes; fortunately we were near enough the same size!

It was at the time of Dorothy's return, that Sadie came with a tale of woe. Her friend, Sarah, who was only sixteen, had got herself into trouble. Her soldier boy-friend, had been posted abroad, and would not be able to let Sarah know his address until he was free to do so. He did not know about the baby. Sarah was sure that he would marry her when he knew that she was pregnant. Sarah's mother and father couldn't stand him, so they had met in secret. Her mother was prim and fussy and her father was an awkward, self-opinionated sort of man. They would kill her, she felt certain, if they found out. Did I know of any ways to get rid of a baby? I didn't, but I promised to ask around. Some weird-and-wonderful remedies were described to me. On the following Saturday afternoon, Sadie said that she would have the house to herself, as her mother was going to Romsey for the day and was not expected back until later that night. We three arranged to meet at Sadie's house at one o'clock when we had finished work. Sadie and I did some rather special shopping beforehand, and when we turned up at her house we found Sarah waiting at the door. As a result of our endeavours, we had one large bottle of gin, two nutmegs, two skipping ropes, and four tins of mustard. We mixed some of the mustard in hot water, and Sarah had to put her feet in it when it was as hot as she could stand. When the beads of perspiration were standing out on her forehead, she was told to skip out in the garden. The second skipping rope was for Sadie, or myself, to keep her company. We took turns in skipping and Sarah put her feet again in to the hot mustard water, until we decided that it was time for her to take the gin. We heated the gin, stirred in two grated nutmegs, and made the poor girl drink it down. Sarah pulled a horrible face, but managed to get it down. Soon after this, she started to alternately laugh and cry. Somebody from next door banged on the wall and we told Sarah to be quiet. She was behaving in a peculiar manner, so we thought that she should have a cup of tea. We gave her a cigarette with it and, the next thing we knew was, she was being violently sick. She was now also sober, so we started the whole process over again. Lord only knows how poor Sarah felt! Both Sadie and I were exhausted after each bout of skipping, but we made Sarah keep at it. She looked so ill by the time evening came, that we thought it wouldn't be long before she had a miscarriage. It was a sorry-looking Sarah who left Sadie's house that night. Whenever I saw Sadie after that, I would ask, 'Any luck for Sarah?' and she would reply, 'No, can't you think of anything else?'

Now I had heard that special tablets could be bought at a certain shop but that they would be expensive. However, we decided to buy them for Sarah. I had to go to the shop to get them, as Sarah was too shy and it was against Sadie's Catholic principles. The next Saturday, after being paid, I went to the shabby little shop which had an equally shabby little man behind the counter. When I, obviously embarassed, asked him if he could help, he gave a sly leer and asked, 'Who's been a naughty girl then, have you got a bun in the oven, darling?' I explained that 'It wasn't for me, it was for my friend' and went bright red. While the odious little man disappeared through a curtain over a door, presumably to get the tablets, I wondered how many other worried and embarrassed females had waited on this side of his counter. He soon returned and placed a small envelope on the counter. 'Here you are, there are twelve pills in there. Do not take more than two, three times a day; and that will be four pounds, please.' Four pounds was more than I or Sadie earned in a week and, although I knew they would be expensive, it still came as a nasty shock. I had four pounds on me, but only just. I gave the pills to Sadie to hand to Sarah, and we waited again for the miracle to happen. The following week I saw Sadie and asked whether there was 'any luck'. 'No, not yet,' was her reply. 'All they did was to make Sarah keep running to the toilet.' We decided that it was a very expensive way of getting diarrhoea. Sarah had been trying other remedies as well, but still had no luck, and the weeks were flying past. When she was six-months' pregnant, in a final, desperate gamble, she asked us to go on a long cycle-ride with her.

Sarah borrowed a man's fixed-wheel drop-handled bike, and we set out early one Sunday morning on a ride to Dorset. We did a total of a hundred and forty miles, there and back, in something like fifteen hours. We were all fairly done in by the time that we arrived back at Northam, and prayed that our gruelling ride might do the trick for Sarah. We waited once more but to no avail. Sarah became almost convinced that nothing was going to happen. She had never had much of a figure, having a plumpish, no-waist body that goes with thick legs. Her mother remarked that Sarah appeared to be putting on weight, but she hadn't, as yet, guessed the reason why. The boy-friend hadn't written and, when I saw Sadie as usual the following Saturday, Sarah was there. In answer to my 'How are you?' she sighed in reply that, 'I've got an awful backache, and I think I must have wind or something, I keep getting pains all across my stomach.' Her complaints rang warning bells in my head, and I persuaded Sarah to go home. Sadie and I went with her and put her to bed, stressing that she would now have to tell her mother. Sarah told us later that she had crawled into her mother's bedroom in the small hours of the following morning and gasped out: 'Mummy, I think I'm having a baby!' Her mother was wonderful and even her father uttered not a word of recrimination. Sarah had a beautiful, healthy child. To finish the story; her boy-friend came home and they were hastily married at a Registry office while the baby remained outside in the pram. So all ended well, in spite of Sadie's and my well-meant, but misguided, help.

XVIII

By the time Ken was seventeen, he had started going out with a regular girl-friend. She was called Ann and was small and fair, with rather an elfin, pretty face, and she seemed very quiet. She liked drawing, and I got on very well with her. Although she was quiet, and seemed shy, she had a strong streak of stubbornness.

She had left her first job in domestic service, where she was very happy, because she could not bring herself to address her employer as 'Madam'. She didn't really want to leave but she couldn't go against her own principles. Ann was a determined little thing, and she made up her mind that the first thing she would buy when she was earning was a sewing machine; and she did just that. Clothes were very hard to come by, for the clothing coupons didn't go very far and making one's own clothes made the coupons last longer. A coat took a large number of coupons. Ann had made a lovely jacket from a grey blanket, but she didn't like it so she gave it to me. I had it for many years, and so I was very pleased to know that Ken had found such a clever girl-friend. People with large families would sell clothing coupons for sixpence or even a shilling a time, and it was nothing for garments to cost 25 per cent more as a result.

Stockings were a terrible problem: fully-fashioned lisle and wool cost about eight shillings a pair, and the first nylons from the States, or Canada, purchased from overseas soldiers or sailors, would cost a pound. Some of those overseas chaps had the strange idea that they could buy a girl for half-a-dozen pairs of nylons. When a cousin of mine was married at the height of the stocking shortage, she borrowed a pair from her friend who had smaller feet. The stockings were so precious that she was warned not to walk in them more than she could help for fear she might make a hole; and that they had to come off straight after the wedding ceremony. The bride confessed that, all through the wedding, rather than concentrating on what she should be doing, she worried about those confounded nylons. Young girls then used 'Miners' leg make-up. The only trouble with it was that if you didn't wash your legs before going to bed, the brown stuff came off on the sheets, to the annoyance of your mother. Can anyone today conceive of paying a quarter of their earnings for a pair of stockings? But that was what a pound was worth in those war-time years of shortage.

We also had dockets for utility furniture. They were only meant for newly-weds or bombed-out families. So many dockets were required for a table, four chairs, a bed and, possibly, a tall-boy or sideboard; anyway, enough for essential furnishing. Those were the days when too much money was chasing too few goods. Second-hand furniture cost the earth; a divan which Mum bought had a nice plain-blue cover which looked as good as new and cost twenty pounds. Mum couldn't understand why, every morning, she found dirt on the floor underneath it. Uncle Joe took the sacking off the bottom to find out why it produced dirt and he found that inside it was packed with old rubbishy rags, sawdust and screwed-up newspapers. Mum went to the shop and demanded her money back. The second-hand dealer told her: 'Hard luck, Madam! I bought it in good faith, the same as you did. Sorry, there's nothing I can do about it.'

When Mum was searching for a pram for her new baby, she found that the utility ones were so poor, with their low chassis, that they conveyed the impression that they had wooden springs as well as wooden wheels. She had to settle for one of them in the end for cheapness sake, as they only cost about four pounds, whereas a second-hand high pram, in good condition, could be as much as twenty to twenty-five pounds. I can remember myself being caught up in the racket. I paid the grocer two bob extra for the privilege of being allowed to buy a bottle of under-the-counter sauce. I was very proud when I took it home in triumph to Mum. I came unstuck, though, with some tea coupons. A girl I knew mentioned to me that she seldom drank her tea ration as she preferred coffee and she left the tea coupons at a certain grocer's shop. I gladly paid her a pound for them, as all I had to do was to go to the grocer's shop once a month and give her name as mine. The snag came when I first tried it. I was told that, 'Mrs Lever took her coupons back as she is moving to another town.' It was all a bit of a disappointment but such happenings were common in war-time.

As the war continued and more glassware and crockery got broken which couldn't be replaced, Mum was only too pleased to buy cups without handles if she was lucky enough to find them. In the pubs, men were even taking jam-jars with them for their beer; they were better than nothing. Beer was occasionally in very short supply so that, when news spread that such-and-such a pub had beer, there was a mad scramble to get to that pub before they were sold out. Uncle Joe used to say that, 'A lot of the beer has arms and legs in it, nowadays,' and he grinned at my puzzled expression. 'Its all right, Nance,' he would continue, 'we strain it through our teeth.' I think he used to call it 'Ullage' which meant that it wasn't clear and it had a lot of bits floating about in it. Uncle liked a drop of whisky now and then, but there was a shortage of that as well so publicans rationed their customers to one tot a person. It was a sad day for Uncle Joe when his favourite pub was demolished by a bomb. The bereaved tone of his voice and his moist-eye might have led one to suppose that it was Winchester Cathedral that had been hit. When we teased him about it, he said that he was a 'Marston man' and that the other beers upset his stomach. For me, however, it wasn't the beer that was a problem but, as usual, the shoes.

I went to London by train for the day with a couple of friends. The first port-of-call for me was Lilley & Skinners, probably the best known shoe-shop in England, all the nobs went there. I bought a pair of very fashionable clogs, which were all the rage then, and they cost me more than a week's wages but lasted for years. Uncle Joe repaired their heels several times, using the mud flap from an Army lorry: 'Such lovely, thick rubber,' he would gloat as he worked away at them. 'Things don't change much, do they Nance,' he would reflect. 'Remember when I used the old leather saddle when you were a kid?' When we had had a look around the shops, we went to Madam Tussaud's and then on to the Windmill Theatre, which had as its proud boast, 'We never close.' It was a wonderful day out. We weren't bothered in London by air-raids, but, when the train arrived at Southampton, it was different; they were certainly getting a basinful of trouble there.

On that night, at the end of November, Southampton had its first sustained raid. There were flares followed by the heavy drone of bombers, which, when they weren't droning, made a throbbing kind of sound. Apparently, it all depended on how high the bombers were. We were told the following day, that 850 tons of heavy explosives and many thousands of incendiary bombs had rained down on Southampton. Thousands of people were homeless and at rest centres, and the drinking water was to be a problem for many days afterwards. We had to fetch it in buckets from an Army water carrier, stationed at the top of our road. Mum told me that, 'When we do get the water turned on again, don't forget to boil it for twenty minutes. Uncle Joe says that the sewage pipes have burst, and that the stuff in them might have got into the tap water. I don't want any of you to get bad stomachs. We've got enough trouble without that.' In addition to the water problem, we had no light, gas or electricity; and such was the extent of the damage to the Gas Works that it had been thought advisable to turn off all gas mains. 'Thank heavens for our old range,' Mum said: 'We are very lucky, you know, lots of poor souls haven't got anything to cook on or to boil a kettle.' And she was genuinely grateful. Later in the same month, from six o'clock until twelve o'clock, there was another heavy raid on Southampton with 950 tons of bombs dropped and 77 people killed. Northam took another heavy pasting with twelve tons of bombs dropped over an area which was only one-sixth of a square mile. There were seven unexploded bombs in the Gasworks.

The war was beginning to have a terrible effect on my stepfather, Bob. The personality of this immaculate, precise and gentle person was beginning to change. Bob had been torpedoed in the Atlantic Ocean in the First World War, and had not been rescued until he had been alone in the water for many hours. The bombing that we were now undergoing was too much for him. All the old memories of his ordeal broke surface and he began to break-up mentally, Mum was now expecting another baby. Bob visibly trembled when the sirens sounded and the fear would cause his bowels to open. He continued working for as long as he was able, but he soon became ill and took to his bed. We had his bed moved downstairs so that he could quickly get to the shelter in the back garden. He began to lock himself away and would only open his door for food, and only go out when he had to collect his weekly sick benefit. He stopped washing, and would not let Mum in to clean the room. Uncle Joe gave Mum extra money for he knew that she was getting little from Bob, and Mum had another little girl. By this time, Bob was so broken in mind that he would push Mum and myself aside (each of us holding one of his children), so as to be first in the shelter when a raid was on. Mum was an intelligent woman and only someone as saintly as she was could have shown such compassion and understanding for her poor, broken husband. The only time Bob now ever really smiled was when he held one of his little girls in his arms.

I later realized what a tower of strength Uncle Joe had been during those wartime years. Whatever Mum would have done without him, I don't know. I wasn't much help for I was as irresponsible as any young teenager can be, living only for the day. I could see the smashed houses and the rubble-lined streets but I felt that was all happening to other people; it wouldn't happen to me, my family, or my house. Some houses in our road were destroyed, but we were among the lucky ones, losing only our windows, and the gaping holes we covered with a sort of webbed cellophane. Even though I knew what bombing was like first-hand at the Black's, it was their house that had gone; I had only lost my job. One morning, when Mum was downstairs seeing to the baby, and getting Uncle Joe off to work, she asked me, 'How you could have slept through all that last night I will never know!' 'Why, was it bad?' I asked. It had been a dreadful night and the rest of the family had spent the night in the shelter, and Mum had given up trying to wake me. She told me that the Germans had been bombing all night; the sound of sirens, ambulances and fire engines lasting until dawn. The sky had apparently glowed an ominous red. I had my morning wash at the kitchen sink, drank my tea, kissed baby on her nose and rushed out of the house. I didn't want to be late for work, so I thought that I would catch a bus. When I reached the top of our road, a large number of people seemed to be about, as the buses couldn't run because of the chaos caused by the night's bombing. Southampton had suffered a saturation raid. I walked along the road, and when we were half-way to the city centre, we were stopped by a warden who told us 'you can't go this way,' and later on by a policeman at another road. 'Sorry,' he said, 'you will have to turn back, the High Street had it last night. It's been wiped out.' Wherever we turned, we were met and sent back by someone in uniform, and we had to make detour after detour. I did, eventually, reach the High Street, or rather what was left of it. A saturation raid usually began after the German 'Pathfinders', who were experienced pilots, had located their targets and dropped chandelier flares which hung over the area to be bombed, causing huge fires which lit the way for the heavy bombers – the cause of the worst destruction. These 'saturation' raids usually lasted till the small hours of the morning.

When I reached what had once been the High Street, all I saw was a mass of smouldering rubble; hardly a shop, or building was left intact. The Bargate, in the centre of this appalling destruction, remained by some miracle, untouched. The fire-hoses were so numerous that they looked like a mass of crazy spaghetti in a canal of muddy soup. All Saints Church had been demolished, and the vaults and crypts below had spewed forth bones, in an indecent manner, on that terrible morning. Weary firemen and wardens, with red-rimmed eyes, worked on, searching for survivors, quenching pockets of fire, and clearing the chaos as best they could.

Mayes was no more; the staff had sheltered that night in the Bargate, whose thick, grey-stone walls had held them safe. Poor Gladys, like everybody else in Mayes that night, escaped wearing only what she stood up in. Gladys didn't believe in banks, and had lost her life savings. I didn't get to work that day. Although I had managed to reach the High Street, I didn't manage to get across it. The horror of it all was beginning to affect me; and I think I grew-up on that morning of vast devastation. In July 1941, Northam was showered by two thousand incendiary bombs. The Gas Works again caught it, and gas was cut off for twenty-four hours. Uncle Joe climbed over the railway wall, and, with buckets of sand and earth, put out two incendiaries which had landed on a heap of coal.

I have only mentioned some of the horrors of the bombing and the terrible times we had to live through; most people could take it– others couldn't, including as I have said, Bob. Later in the war there were parachute-mines, which wiped out a dozen houses at a go and, at the very end, the flying bombs. We would bend our heads back to search the sky when we heard the sound of one of their engines, which sounded like a two-stroke motor-cycle. Short flames belched from the tail and everyone would pray that it would go on and not stop overhead. Once the engine stopped, the bomb might land very near. It was, then, perfectly normal for us to hope that it would pass on and, if need be, kill somebody else, but not us. This would also be our feeling when the drone of heavy German bombers was overhead: 'Some poor devil's going to get it,' we would say. The Luftwaffe, at the very least, did slum clearance work in Northam; only our own small side of Northam remained relatively unscathed. The other side of Northam Road, which included most of the district to its boundary at the River Itchen, was almost completely destroyed.

Shopping for food was a nightmare; we had to queue for every-thing. I once stood for two hours in a seemingly endless queue to get five pounds of potatoes and I fainted; not, however, before I had got them. It was at this time that a store called Edwin Jones, would be having a few dolls in for Christmas. These dolls had hard-paste faces and cloth bodies and limbs, but dolls were scarce – even second-hand ones could not be had – so one Saturday I joined the early morning queue, at five-thirty a.m., and, after a four-hour wait, got my reward. The doll was for my little sister, and was her first. The long wait had been well worth it when I saw her face as she opened her presents on Christmas morning. Mum, like all other housewives, worked miracles with the rations. We didn't throw much away in the pig-bin at the end of our road. Each road had a pig-bin and the food was collected daily from it. Sometimes, we had a delicious rabbit stew. Uncle Joe kept rabbits in the garden. Mum would gratefully accept carrot peelings and cabbage leaves which neighbours left at our front door for our rabbits. The smell of fried onions often greeted us when we arrived home for dinner. Mum was a great one for them and, even if we only had mashed potatoes with them, they were at least tasty. Our onions and potatoes occasionally came from Uncle Joe's allotment, but he never grew enough for us hungry children, and one of his jokes was to suggest that I had hollow legs. It was the meat that was Mum's biggest problem. At our lowest point of rationing, we were down to eightpence-worth of meat and fourpence-worth of corned beef for each person.

One night, when we were in the shelter, the thuds of bombs and roars of explosions seemed close. 'My God, that was a near one,' Mum said. 'Did you feel that?' We all had felt it and, in the morning, we discovered that houses about six doors up had 'had it', as it was termed. In our front bedroom, a big lump of masonry, some cubic foot in size, had come through the roof and onto the bed. After that, we seemed to spend every night in the shelter and it was astonishing that any of us managed to get any sleep. The shelter was so over-crowded that it was like sleeping in a dog kennel. The Anderson shelter, which was what we had, was issued to people with back gardens, although some people erected their shelters in the front garden, disguised by a rockery on top. 'The Shelter' was, in most cases, made of heavy-duty galvanized iron; the sides consisted of three sheets each six-feet long and curved at the top so as to meet the other and form a roof. The back end sheets were six-feet long, and the smaller sheets top and bottom in the centre of the front left enough room for us to get in and out. The structure stood in an iron channel to keep it firm, and had angle-iron supports about halfway up inside. The completed shelter was about six-feet high, six-feet long and four-feet wide. Uncle Joe worked hard to make our Anderson as comfortable as he could. He put two narrow bunks on each side and gave the inside a coat of distemper. The condensation was a nuisance but he couldn't do much about that. A small stool between the two-tier bunks at the end opposite the entrance completed the furnishings. People who didn't have gardens were issued with Morrison Shelters, which were a sort of steel box with mesh sides, and could be used as a table; they were supposed to withstand a house collapsing on them. Finally, of course, there were the street shelters, some of which took up most of the pavement room. I managed to get a splendid black-eye from one of them during the blackout. We could all get about fairly well by using the outline of houses against the sky to give us our bearings on the darker nights. Some people took torches, often dimmed, which they flicked on and off. Most of the street shelters had a tiny red light outside. As I was hurrying home one particular night, I spied a tiny red light bobbing towards me through the pitch-darkness. Suddenly, 'Bump', and I saw stars. It wasn't, in fact, a little red light bobbing towards me, but me bobbing up and down as I ran smack into a street shelter!

XIX

Now that Uncle Joe was earning good money, he began to go out more frequently. He was glad to get away from Bob as much as anything, as he didn't have Mum's patience where Bob was concerned; indeed, he thought that Mum was far too soft with him. Uncle Joe's particular friend had a wife, Ivy, which, of all names, was the one most hated by Mum. Uncle Joe used to take her out, having got, of course, her husband's permission. The three of them became quite inseparable. Mum thought that they only used Uncle Joe and she resented the way he poured his money out on gin for Ivy. For Uncle Joe, it was the start of a friendship that was to last many years. Ivy was a gay and sparkling woman, who took to calling for Uncle Joe in the evening. Mum actually kept her waiting outside the front door and did not invite her in. Such behaviour from Mum of all people was astonishing; the only other person she had ever treated in this manner was, as I have said, Sadie. Uncle Joe remonstrated with Mum, saying that she was unfair to Ivy, but Mum never relented; she just couldn't stand her, or her name. Ivy stopped calling at our house, although her friendship with Uncle Joe continued but, when Ivy's house was bombed,

Mum made room upstairs for what bits and pieces had been
salvaged from the wreck until Ivy found a new house. There were
to be plenty of empty houses to choose from in Southampton, once
the bombing really got under way.

Now that Uncle Joe had his new friends, politics took a back
seat. He only had one antagonist – the German. Being able to work
again, and his warden's duties, had made a new man of Uncle Joe.
Give him the tools, indeed, and he would finish the job! Uncle was
so fiercely patriotic.

Dorothy joined the Girls' Training Corps when she was fifteen.
The age for joining was supposed to be sixteen, but Dorothy was
such a well-developed girl that it was easy to get away with the
small discrepancy in age. Their uniform was a white shirt, black
tie, skirt, shoes and beret. It was a civilian movement, a sort of
glorified Girl Guides. They were supposed to help during air raids
by taking messages by cycle, if the Post Office telephone wires were
put out of action, or to look after children, and in general to make
themselves useful. The Commander-in-Chief was a high official of
the W.R.N.S., and, on a certain day, there was to be a parade of
the Southampton section of the Corps in front of the Civic Centre.
Dorothy took great pains to look her very smartest; they were
going to have their pictures on the front page in the *Echo*. The
parade took place on the appointed day. The cameras whirled as
several high dignitaries inspected the girls; Dorothy was in the
front rank at the end. That evening, when the *Echo* came out,
Dorothy was among the first in the queue, for we were all dying to
see her picture on the front page. There, indeed was the picture, a
beautiful picture, but they had cut Dorothy out. When she received
her postcard picture of the parade, it was fairly apparent why they
had snipped her off. Dorothy's figure was, without a shadow of
doubt, superb. Her bust measured forty-four inches, her waist
eighteen inches and her hips thirty-six inches. Standing to attention with the other girls, with her shoulders back and her chest out,
Dorothy made the rest of them look flat-chested so, for the sake of
uniformity, she had been chopped off. In Dorothy's picture, the
Commander-in-Chief was there and so were two officers from the
Royal Navy, both grinning in admiration at Dorothy's magnificent
posture.

One morning, when I was standing at the bus stop waiting to go to

Myself at nineteen in a boilersuit straight from work in the
auxiliary workshop

work, an ex-school friend of mine, Lily, asked, 'Why don't you come to our place of work. I get twenty-five shillings a week.' 'That's good,' I replied, 'I only get fifteen shillings at Pirelli's. Where do you work?' Lily told me she worked in an Army Auxiliary Workshop. 'It's smashing there,' she assured me, 'you'll love it.' The next day, I took the afternoon off and applied for a job, and was told that I could start straight away. Another ten-bob a week! All I had to do now was to give in my notice. I had not realized that, as a wartime measure, one couldn't just leave a job and my boss at Pirelli's told me firmly, 'No, you cannot leave, and that is final!' I proceeded to make his life a misery. I was rude to him, I cheeked him, and even swore at him. I kept this up for a whole week, until he couldn't stand it any longer and finally sacked me. I had got what I wanted; there's more than one way of skinning a cat!

I loved it in the Workshop, although it was a bit of a blow to find that I should have to spend some of my precious clothing coupons on two boiler-suits. That is what we girls wore; they had a flap at the back like the old-fashioned combinations which elderly women wore as an under-garment. We learned to repair radiators with a soldering iron and even to do some welding. I did not escape the attentions of the male instructor here, who, when he was showing me what to do, would stand behind me and put his arms over mine. 'No, not like that,' he'd say, 'you've got the flame too near the metal.' I thought he pressed unnecessarily close to me. We camouflage-painted Army vehicles of every size. It was nothing to see a dozen women of all ages in the road with their paint pots, standing on vehicle bonnets to reach the top of the cabs, climbing like monkeys, as they covered the canopy irons with dirty greens and browns, or lying underneath vehicles to get at the chassis and petrol tank. The troop-carriers were so big that we often worked in pairs on them. We had to clean them first, of course, and that meant jacking them up to get the wheels off. Some of the smaller girls were dwarfed by them, but they took it all in their stride, and worked away singing the current hit-song at the top of their voices. When an air-raid had started, most of us made a beeline for the inspection pits, and cowered beneath a lorry, until one of the more intelligent men noticed that his head was only about a foot away from the petrol tank. At this discovery, we ran for the street-shelter, which was not far from the workshop. We usually worked twelve hours a day. The work was urgent, urgent, urgent! The army were waiting for vehicles, we were told, and one of the foremen was constantly urging us to 'Get Cracking'. How I remember those words! We heard them first thing in the morning, after tea-break, after dinner, after a ten-minute stop at five o'clock; in fact all the time. He was an old-fashioned foreman and they don't breed them like him anymore. We were often indescribably dirty; what with the burning-off of paint, and the cleaning underneath of vehicles with wire-brushes and paraffin. We had, it should be realized, no rubber gloves issued to us. I thought that the money was tremendous, not that there was much to spend it on, but, with all the overtime, I earned as much as four pounds a week. There were not many young men working with us, for most of them had been called up, and the young men that we did have were exempted owing to poor eyesight, bad hearts, or some other valid medical reason.

Dorothy came to work there, but had not been working very long when she fell ill with suspected T.B. and for a year had to become a home convalescent. It meant more strain on poor Mum, who already had enough worry and trouble. Dorothy was allowed an extra ration of milk, butter and eggs. I was allowed a pint of milk a day at the workshop but, of course, I didn't drink it there; each day, I took it home for Mum. But it wasn't all work; we laughed, and joked, and enjoyed ourselves. The little shop around the corner was owned by an eccentric old woman, and one day, when a crowd of us were working in the road, some German Luftwaffe prisoners-of-war came marching along under military escort. The old lady came out of her shop and waved to them, calling out, 'God bless you my lads.' She was harmlessly potty. We all laughed at her, and gave both her and the Germans several 'Heil Hitler' salutes. The Germans looked quite puzzled as they marched by; the silly incident amused us for the rest of the afternoon.

Dorothy went to live at Aunt Bell's at Shirley, as Ken had married Ann, and they were expecting a baby. Nobody minded moving to my Aunt Bell's – it was pure pleasure to live with her. Aunt Bell's first husband had died when I was a child and her new husband was quite a one for the gay life. Aunt Bell, like Mum, had been out to work for as long as I could remember, and was as soft with her money as her husbands. When I went to visit her one day we naturally turned to the subject of Northam and its people. I knew that she missed being away and loved a little pleasant gossip. 'Have you seen anything of the Carters?' she asked. The Carters were a family who had lived in Guildford Street, where Aunt Bell had lived as a child. A family called Monk had also lived in the same street. 'Yes,' I replied, 'one of the Carters is marrying a Monk.' 'What's that you say about marrying a Monk?' asked Aunt Bell. 'Yes,' I raised my voice, 'one of the Carters is marrying a Monk.' 'Well, I'll be blowed,' she said, 'I didn't think that monks were allowed to get married.' Dorothy and I exchanged glances and smiled. After all, Aunt Bell was getting on a bit. She grinned then at us in her old conspiratorial manner and chuckled like a two-year-old. She had been having us on.

After a while Ken, who was still in the Navy, found a house for Ann and the baby, so Dorothy returned home. When any of us brought friends home, we would casually explain that Bob was mad, and that if he came into the room and looked odd, or did anything strange, not to take any notice of him. We were all so used to living with him that we saw nothing strange in the situation. We all began to treat him like an invisible man. Once Dorothy brought a friend home called Joan. Soon, the three of us were fiddling with hair-styles and make-up, and Joan was trying on my lipstick in front of the mirror when Bob entered. His braces were dangling down the back of his trousers, his open shirt revealed a filthy vest and, unwashed and unshaven, he stopped behind Joan and stared at her. Then he began verbal abuse pointing with his dirty, shaking finger at Joan who was a 'Painted Whore', a 'Harlot', 'a Jezebel'; Biblical quotations flowed, mixed in with filthy language. It was the nightmare situation that Dorothy and I had always feared. Joan didn't know what to do. When Bob went back to his room, she started to giggle, partly to cover her embarrassment, and partly to show that she was an adult who could take such oddities in her stride: 'Silly old bugger,' she said. Mum had heard Joan swear. We didn't swear in our house, which seemed an odd thing with Bob behaving as he did, but we still didn't swear in our house. 'It's no laughing matter. Two wrongs don't make a right,' Mum snapped at Joan. 'He doesn't know what he's saying, and you do.' That was that! Dorothy and Joan stayed friends, but Joan never came to our house again. Mum, in the old days, would have been apologetic and lightly passed over the incident, but now her nerves were drawn as tight as a bow-string; she couldn't take much more. Joan's father came to the house to have it out with Bob, and Mum had to explain the whole sorry business. Joan's father left, saying that he just wouldn't put up with it; he would get something done about Bob.

We tried to keep some semblance of sanity at home, and, at Christmas and on Bob's birthday, we each made an effort to give him a present of some kind; usually an article of clothing or some tobacco. But it was a waste of time and effort, for the present would disappear to his room and not be seen again. Bob was like a squirrel hoarding nuts for the winter – except that for him winter never came; time for him had no season or reason. Bob had very painful piles, Mum told me, and this was another reason why we should all show him more sympathy. Well, his piles must have been bad because, after a visit to the Doctor, he was admitted very quickly into hospital, which gave Mum an opportunity to get into his room. It was obvious why he had been giving Mum so little money; stuffed in a hole in the mattress was over forty pounds. The room was in a terrible condition. It took Mum and Uncle Joe a whole week to clean. When Bob returned from hospital, his behaviour deteriorated. The authorities were too overburdened for Mum to get any help; nobody would listen to her. Bob began to smear the walls with his own excrement and was even filthier in his appearance. He also exposed himself on the rare occasions he left his room. Bob became a figure of fun for the children of our street, picking up dog-ends from the pavement and talking to himself. Still Mum, wonderful Mum, showed her compassion for him.

Bob did many strange things to gain sympathy. Although he had a fire in his room, for a short while he took to sitting in a pub in the evening, where he would light a candle at which he warmed his hands, rubbing his fingers together as if they were frozen. If the pub customers felt in a generous mood they would buy Bob a pint and, when he became too much of a nuisance and was asked to leave, he would simply move on to another pub. Mum almost begged him to wear the new boots which she had bought, but although he took them, he continued to wear his down-trodden and shabby, almost sole-less, shoes. When Mum asked him why he wasn't wearing his new boots, he replied that he had lost them. Since Mum couldn't get into his room to check, she bought him another pair. He took those from her, but never wore them. When Dorothy came into the front room one Sunday afternoon, she was surprised to find Bob there, he pushed her aside and left the room. There was a smell of burning. Dorothy went to the fireplace and found in it half-burnt remains of cards and papers of hers. When she confronted Bob with them, he rushed into the garden and, taking up one of the toy tricycles which belonged to one of his own children, screwed it into a tangle of metal. Bob was surprisingly strong. The meek and sorry exterior which he showed to the outside world was very different from the difficult and violent man who lived in our house. Bob even used to have the extra rations meant for Dorothy. Mum couldn't keep her eye on him all the time, and he would think nothing of cooking himself eggs and bacon, or anything else that was going, in the small hours of the morning. For Mum, it was an unending and unequal battle. People were forever coming to her with tales of Bob's odd behaviour, and everyone who knew her sympathized with her terrible problem. On the other hand, there were those people who did not, and who felt sorry for Bob, which was exactly what his own tortured self most wanted. We were never allowed to grumble too fiercely about him to Mum, although among ourselves, we most certainly did.

XX

One day when I arrived home from work, I found Mum in bed upstairs and Dorothy looking after the children. Dorothy was at home because she had a sore throat. There was no coal and the house was cold. Mum was shivering in bed with a severe chill. She must have felt very ill to have gone to bed at all. When Uncle Joe came home, I said, 'Can't we get some coal from somewhere and put a fire in Mum's room?' 'You know what your Mum is like, Nance,' Uncle replied, 'She would rather freeze than borrow.' Suddenly, images of all the lumps of coal littering the railway lines behind our house flashed through my mind. Some of the coal had been there for years, having fallen off the high-piled trucks when they were shunted. So far as I knew, no-one had ever nipped over the wall to pinch any, which was just what I was going to do. I went out to the garden and climbed up on the top of the shelter, cocked one leg over the wall and then the other. It was pitch-black. There was a drop on the other side of the wall of some ten feet.

I let the rest of myself over and, hanging on by my fingers and then dropping down, I picked myself up, then I gathered up the lumps of coal and threw them over into our garden, silently praying that nobody would hear. When I thought that I had enough coal, I tried to get back but it was hopeless. I knew that if I went a little along the track I could climb over a ten foot gate into our road; so I set off. I fell down several times on my unfamiliar path and, when I heard voices, I hid behind a huge pile of coal. Eventually, I got there and scaled the gate to freedom. When I entered the house, I was greeted by astonished looks from both Dorothy and Uncle Joe. 'Good God, where have you been?' Uncle asked. 'Why?' I replied defensively. 'Have a look at yourself in the mirror,' Uncle said. I had to laugh at myself, for the mirror showed that I was as black as a coalman. 'You had better wash yourself before your Mother sees you, and don't let her know where you have been either,' Uncle warned. I had been waiting for him to tell me off, but he didn't. I didn't care, anyway, I wasn't going to let Mum be cold with all that coal going to waste on the other side of the wall. I had a quick wash in the sink with cold water, and hurried upstairs to light a fire in Mum's room. There was a lovely blaze going in no time at all. As I was leaving Mum asked, 'Where did you get the coal from Nance?' 'At the back of the cupboard, Mum,' I replied. 'Come here by the bed and look at me,' she ordered. I turned around and looked her full in the face. 'I know where it came from,' she said with that peculiar little smile of hers. 'And I know that you meant well, but don't ever do it again.' I left the room without feeling guilty, and I knew that I would do it again for Mum if occasion demanded. I wondered how Mum had guessed but, when I looked in the mirror downstairs, it was obvious. My quick wash had not included my eyes. I had two beautiful, round black patches there.

That winter before Christmas, I had a bad cough so Mum pushed her two babies in the pram to my work place and produced a bottle of cough mixture and a spoon; I had to stand there and take my medicine. I was seventeen years old, but she had been worried by hearing me cough away all night long.

Mum listened eagerly when it was announced on the radio that whale steaks would soon be available in the fish shops. The Ministry of Food stated that if the whale steak was given a little onion-flavour we would hardly tell it from the real thing. The daily papers splashed out with their own recipes. Mum bought a piece of the dark-red coarse-grained meat, cut it into small cubes, and boiled it with onions to make a pie-filling. The smell of the whale was hardly appetizing but when the pie was ready for the table, its lovely, golden pastry promised high hopes of a good meal. The 'pretend-pie', however, was a ghastly flop. We all agreed that it was the nearest one could get to a cod-liver oil pie, and the odour of the whale meat ruined the vegetables. I, who could eat anything, failed with whale meat.

Now that the tide of war was turning in our favour, the drone of bombers overhead made sweet music to our ears; they were going the other way. London, of course, was still suffering from the rockets; I heard it said that they looked like telegraph poles coming down from the sky. We would look up and beam at the American Flying Fortresses carrying their block-busters into enemy-occupied France. At this time, square-tin canisters appeared on street corners, and strange symbols were painted on the walls beside them. We soon knew what they were intended for as the Army carried out a smoke-making rehearsal, and the resultant smell was not exactly like Eau-de-Cologne. We now know that the purpose behind the smoke screen was to conceal troop movements, for Southampton was one of the major embarkation ports for the Normandy landings. Now that the worst seemed over, Mum desperately hoped that Bob would get better, but he did not. He went out at night more often, after carefully locking his door behind him. Flats and houses which had been empty were now beginning to be occupied as people drifted back into Southampton. It was then that I left home.

I still knew, of course, of Mum's plight with Bob. Mum, at long last, felt desperate enough to call in the Health Inspector, a young woman. Bob let her into his room and, with all the cunning of the mad, promised to open his window and let Mum wash his clothes and clean his room. He even promised to wash himself and get his hair cut for, by now, the children of the road were calling him 'Jesus' because of his long hair and beard. The Health Inspector left and, as soon as the door closed behind her, Bob came out with every filthy word he could think of.

The war had just finished when Mum's friendly neighbour called to say that she was sorry for her, but that she would have to report Bob for exposing himself to one of her little girls. Bob was sent to prison. Mum's cup of misery, however, was not yet full. John was now back from Dorset and the two little girls were at school. Uncle Joe was still giving Mum extra money but, even so, she took what cleaning-work which she could do and still be back in time for the children when they came home from school. When Bob was released from prison, he was at least clean, but still did not behave rationally. He did not stay clean for long, however, and reverted to his former dirty habits. He went out once a week to get his dole money and would place one pound on the table for Mum. He still kept his door locked and rarely spoke. Mum was still trying to get help, both for Bob and herself. Yet the Authorities persistently turned a deaf ear to her appeals for help. Bob was keeping a bucket in his room for toilet purposes and, if he heard strange voices, deliberately came through the living room with it. One day Mum came home from work a little late, to find the girls already back from school. Bob had the eldest girl in his room on his bed with him. I don't suppose that there was any harm done, but Mum could not trust him. Only she knew what a desperately mentally sick man he was. As a last resort, she consulted a solicitor, in the belief that if she could get a divorce, she would be able to get Bob away from the house and possibly put in care. The solicitor asked 'Why do you want a divorce. Do you want to get married again?' At this, Mum broke down, and cried. She poured out all her fears to him. Not all solicitors are hard, money-grabbing men, and this one listened, much moved by what he heard. He told Mum to go home and that help would be on the way. The telephone wires in that man's office must have burnt red-hot, for on the same afternoon, two Health Officers arrived at our house and removed Bob to an asylum, where he remained until he died fifteen years later.

When Uncle Joe and Mum opened Bob's room, they found the wall-cupboards full of bags and tins of dog-ends. There were dozens of pairs of shoes, which sympathetic people had given him. Under the bed were jackets and coats, once again, probably given to him by people who thought he was a tramp. The bed mattress concealed sixty pounds and some thousand fleas. All that could be burnt, including the mattress, blankets and Bob's clothes, were taken out into the garden. Paraffin was poured over them and they were burnt. Mum always said that the war was to blame for Bob's decline. 'Everybody has their weak spots,' she would say. 'With some it's their chest or their back or their bones, with Bob it was his nerves. He was a fine man until the bombing started, it was just too much for him. At least he will get all the help now that I couldn't give him, and I can go to work without worrying myself sick.' Mum now had peace, at least for a while.

XXI

I first met Fred when I was nearly seventeen. He was small, dark, vital, black hair swept back from his high intelligent forehead; he had a no-nonsense face. Fred was a man's man, and nobody would lightly tangle with him. I was still going out with other boys and tried to hide this from him but Fred always found out. We sometimes used to meet in a pub where a rather amusing episode occurred. I was still very green and, as we sat drinking our brown ale at our table – I thought I was being very mature – a girl across the room took my eye. She was one of our older Northam girls, not much older than me, about twenty, I should think. I smiled and she smiled back. Fred trod heavily on my foot under the table, and I asked him 'What did you do that for?' 'That's a prostitute,' he hissed, as if she was the lowest of the low. I had never had a prostitute pointed out to me before, and had often wondered what they looked like. I looked at her again and then at Fred. 'Don't be so silly,' I expostulated, 'She's one of the girls from Northam. She used to go to our School. Her sister was in my class.' Fred sighed at my ignorance. 'Drink up, we are leaving,' was all he said.

We became more than good friends, as the saying is, and the time came when I realized that I was pregnant. I hugged my miserable secret to myself, and tried to do all the things that Sadie and I had previously done to the unfortunate Sarah – with about as much success. It didn't show for months, being hidden by my dungarees and short jacket, and I was able to go on working – being discreetly sick each morning with the occasional fainting. Sadie was also pregnant, but she had married her Canadian Air Force boy-friend and was looking forward to going to live in Canada after the war. Mum must have sensed that I was miserable about something, for one day, when I was four-months pregnant, she came upstairs to me as I lay in bed. I had been crying, and sat up when Mum came in. I blurted out all my troubles to her. She put

Corner of Radcliffe Road showing the gasometer

her arms around me and cradled my tear-stained face against her soft, warm breast. She comforted me by saying: 'It's not the end of the world, my love, there are worse things in life than having a baby, and you don't have to get married if you don't want to.' She tucked me up in bed as if I were a small child, and kissed me. 'Have a nice sleep now, Nance,' she said, 'Life goes on, and you will learn to accept it.' I continued working until I was eight months' gone. Because of the severe bombing, all expectant mothers were sent out of Southampton to have their babies. There were two places they were sent to, a 'Folly Farm' somewhere in the country, and to a mansion called Oakley House, Abingdon, Berkshire. I was sent there. We went about two weeks before our babies were due and it was so quiet and peaceful there. For a whole month, I heard not a siren, nor felt the shakings of a bombing raid. I still hadn't made up my mind what I wanted to do, and Fred brought Dorothy on his motorbike to see me. My son was born on

a gale-swept night in March. I was eighteen; as I held the tiny
thing in my arms, I wondered why I had tried so hard to be rid of
him. He was the spitting-image of Fred. After two weeks, I was
allowed home and then looked around for a part-time job. I wanted
to breast-feed my baby as Mum had done. I got a job as an usher-
ette in the Plaza Cinema, which was virtually at the end of our road.
The cinema has long since gone, to be replaced by the Southern
Television Centre. The money wasn't very good and a friend told
me about a working-man's café in Northam Road which apparently
needed a waitress. The hours were staggered, which would suit me,
and, although the wages were not very good, my friend said that
the tips were excellent. I applied for the job and was taken on to
start in a week's time. The tips were not quite as good as my friend
had led me to suppose but, even so, I enjoyed myself there. I
sometimes served behind the counter and the staff had a free
daily-dinner. I stayed at the café for four months. The most
remarkable thing about it was it's sheer cleanliness. The owner was
Greek or Maltese, I'm not quite sure which now, but I do know
that he was extremely fastidious and watched to make sure that we
all washed our hands when returning from the lavatory. Our hair
was to be kept covered up in his kitchen; the male cook wore a
white hat and his female helpers a scarf. On a wall inside the
dining room was a large notice: PATRONS OF THIS CAFE ARE WELCOME
TO INSPECT MY KITCHEN AT ANY TIME and the owner's signature was
on the bottom right hand corner.

It was unfair of me to dump yet another baby on Mum. She had
enough to do, what with Uncle Joe, and Dorothy, and now my two
little sisters. Sylvia, the elder, was a darling, with dimpled cheeks,
a head of burnished copper curls, and was no bother at all. She
slept all night and played all day. Sandra, the other one, was quite
different, she was a wilful child in every way. From an early age
she dominated Sylvia. The two girls have always felt a special tie
with each other, rather like Dorothy and myself. Uncel Joe hadn't
said much to me since I had my baby, but he played with him as he
did with Sandra and Sylvia, and indeed with all children. Now and
then, he would say to me, in a gruff voice, 'All right, Nance?' and
I would reply, 'Yes, fine Uncle.' I finally made up my mind about
Fred. I, and baby, moved in with him in his flat in Shirley, a quiet
district of Southampton, near the beautiful Common. We were
later married. I still used to push the baby to Northam, 'Home' as

I always called it, almost every day, to see Mum. Fred used to ask, 'What do you want to go down that dump for? You've got a lovely home here, with carpets on the floor, and nice furniture. I can't understand you.'

The years passed by and Ken and Ann had three children. Dorothy married a nice boy; John was married; and Uncle Joe was still going out with Ivy, whose husband had now died and so poor Uncle Joe thought that his chance had come. Ivy, to his disappointment, married someone else, and Uncle Joe continued, as before, to be spare man, paying in gin for the pleasure of Ivy's company.

Mum was still working to support her two daughters and Uncle Joe stayed on with her. Although Bob had been in the mental hospital for many years, Mum received no state help at all, and was feeling very down and tired. I didn't know she had cancer of the breast. She never complained, or told anybody except my Aunt Flo, who later told me that she had persuaded Mum to go to the Public Assistance to see if she could get help. Mum went, together with Aunt Flo. Mum later told me that she shook and trembled when speaking to the smart young man at the counter, and could only stammer out that she needed financial help. After listening to her, the young man asked whether Mum had ever considered getting a job. Mum felt sick with embarassment and dismay at this question. She couldn't speak, and fled from the building as if chased by the devil. She knew that she had to go into hospital to have her breast removed but she told no-one, except Uncle Joe and Aunt Flo. They were asked to say nothing about it to any of us children.

Mum worked till eight o'clock that night at the St Michael's Lodging House, where she worked as a cleaner. It was bitterly cold and snowing. An old tramp lay dying in one of the side rooms as the Hospital wouldn't admit him. A doctor had been in to see him and had left a prescription. Nobody would go to the chemist and get the medicine for the old tramp. Mum was moved by his plight so she took his prescription to an all-night chemist in the High Street, and returned with the medicine for him. By the time she had done all that, the snow was thicker than ever, and the buses had stopped running. She didn't get home that night till after ten. The following morning she was admitted into hospital for her operation.

Uncle Joe came up to let us know that the operation had been

done. He said that the girls could look after themselves; Sylvia was
working and Sandra was fourteen. It was arranged that Mum
would come and stay with me during her convalescence. When I
saw her in hospital I chided her for not letting us know: 'I didn't
want to worry you,' she replied. Mum stayed with us for a month
while she convalesced but was eager to get back to the girls and
Uncle Joe, although they protested to her that they were managing
splendidly on their own. Mum now got a small allowance from the
Government, and was convinced that she would soon be well
enough to return to work. She did look well, and Mum was ever
full of hope. She returned to Northam and I went to see her nearly
every day, taking my little girl with me. Every time I asked Mum
how she was she would reply: 'I'm fine, don't worry so, Nance.'

That Autumn, Fred said to me: 'I want you to come and look
at a house with me. It's in a bad condition and is going cheap. I
thought that we might get a mortgage if you like it.' The house was
not far from where we lived; it was a barn of a place, with a good-
sized garden. Fred was enthusiastic. 'It's structurally sound,' he
told me, and I knew that he had fallen in love with the place. Our
two children could have their own bedroom. The flat where we
were living had only three rooms and a kitchen, together with a
bathroom. It also meant that I would have to go to work, and I was
now thirty-one.

We managed to get a mortgage and moved in. My son, David,
and his friend, both thirteen year-olds, carted a ton of coal over in
a barrow to our new home, pushing it to and fro, until it had all
been transferred. I had only just had it delivered to the flat and
couldn't afford to leave it behind. Dorothy had recently had a baby
boy, and she, together with her husband and baby, came to live in
a flat upstairs, which meant that someone would be able to keep an
eye on my little girl when she came home from school.

I was now working full-time in a factory. Then we realized that
Mum's illness had started again. She came to live with us, staying
upstairs with Dorothy during the day and sitting downstairs with
Fred and myself in the evenings. The two girls came with her.
Mum's illness got progressively worse, until she eventually had to
stay in bed. Dorothy nursed her with her usual saintly devotion.
Nothing was too much bother for us where Mum was concerned,
and when I came home from work each night, I cooked for the
six of us, did my bits and pieces, and then saw to Mum's washing.

There were always two or three sheets and as many nightdresses. Dorothy had to work hard at keeping Mum dry and sweet-smelling; bedsores are a terrible thing once you let up.

I asked Fred if he thought that we could get a television set for Mum. He immediately took the one which we had and that same night put it in her room. He bought another set for us later. Mum read the complete works of Shakespeare during her illness and, one day, mentioned pointedly to me that if anything should happen to her, she wished to donate the cornea of her eyes to enable some other unfortunate to read. Mum had never had the time to read before, and she derived great pleasure from Shakespeare.

Mum was almost pitifully grateful for what she had. We all spoke cheerfully about the time when she would get better, although, in our hearts, we knew that this was the end. We bought her the most magnificent red dressing-gown we could find, and a pair of gloriously-gaudy slippers for the time when she would be able to walk again. We hung the dressing-gown on her bedroom door so she could see it, as if it was just waiting for her to be well enough to put it on. People who mouth pious platitudes about the sanctity of human life, usually do so at a safe distance. Are they the ones who, day-by-day and night-by-night, try gently to turn over an anguished body? Are they the ones who have to look away when the doctor practises his refined torture of trying to find somewhere to put his hyperdermic syringe, when most of what remains is but a living skeleton. And, then, for Mum the final degredation, of lying in her own mess, and having to ask to be washed.

Towards the end, the District Nurse came each day, as did the doctor. They kept saying that Mum couldn't go on much longer, but she did. She went on, and on, and on. I virtually asked the doctor if he could end it all, but he said that he was doing what he could to relieve her pain, more than that, he would not do. If I could have put Mum out of her misery, I would have done so with a clear conscience, and without any compunction whatsoever. I have never wavered from this thought; I wouldn't have let the lowliest animal suffer for as long as Mum suffered. I began to sleep on the floor of her room to be near if she needed me; and then I would go on to work in the mornings. One morning, I got a phone call from Dorothy. It was over at last. I came straight home and looked down at what had once been my lovely, warm, kindest-hearted Mum, and I was suddenly reminded of that time in the hospital, all those years ago, when I had walked into the ward and not recognized her. What was lying on her bed did not seem to be at all like the Mum I had known. She was only fifty-four, such a short time to have lived and so much of it had been hard.

She wasn't finished with this world yet. She still had something to give, and I knew what I had to do. I 'phoned the Eye Hospital and told them of her wish, adding, 'I think you should know that she died of cancer. Does it make any difference?' Apparently, there would be no ill effects on the cornea, they said, and they would send a man up within the hour. He came, carried out the essentials, and thanked us for letting them know so promptly. Mum's last request had been carried out.

I didn't think that I would ever stop hurting inside after that day, but, of course, I did. Everybody suffers the same trauma at some time or other but as Mum had so often said to me in the past, 'Life goes on, Nance.'

EPILOGUE

First Sandra, and later, Sylvia, left. They are now both married with children. Uncle Joe lived on his own at 'home' for a few more years, until Aunt Bell and her invalid husband, now retired, joined him. Her husband had become an irritable, bad-tempered and quarrelsome invalid, who had Aunt Bell waiting on him hand-and-foot, in spite of the fact that she herself could only walk with a stick. She had broken her hip while shopping in the snow having gone out to get groceries for an old lady across the way who was housebound. Aunt Bell had worked full-time until she reached seventy but she never thought of herself as the old lady that she was. Uncle Joe and her husband weren't particularly fond of each other and it finally boiled up to a great row. Uncle Joe was driven from the house where he had been so important a figure for so many years. Aunt Bell didn't want him to go, for he was still her youngest brother, but Uncle Joe had had enough.

He thought that he would go to Ivy's and that she would be pleased to have him. For all those years he had been Ivy's faithful shadow and, very deaf and nearly blind, Uncle Joe took himself off to his oldest remaining friend. He had not been there for many weeks when he accidentally overheard Ivy say, 'Well, what can I do? I don't want to be stuck with a blind old man.' Uncle Joe was cut to the quick. 'Don't worry,' he told Ivy, 'You won't be stuck with me any longer.' He went straight off to the Sailors' Home, which took him in as he had served in the Royal Navy. From there, Uncle Joe moved to an Old People's home where he was very comfortable. It was there that I started to visit him almost once a fortnight; Dorothy and Sandra also visited him there.

I had a mini-van then, and I used to take him out in it. He was so shaky on his feet that he couldn't walk very well, and it used to take about ten minutes to get him from the door of the Home to my waiting van. I did my best to take him to a different place and he waited for my visits with child-like eagerness. Once, I took him to see Aunt Flo, who lived in a mixed Old People's home, and the two old people wept as they embraced. Aunt Flo still had those lively black-button eyes, which were very much in evidence as she and Uncle Joe talked of the old days. The two of them even became excited at a plan they had concocted to see if Uncle could obtain a transfer to Aunt Flo's home. At his request, but reluctantly, I took him to see Ivy. She wasn't at home and, although Uncle Joe was disappointed, he said 'We'll try again another time.' We tried three more times, but Ivy was never there. As we travelled all over Southampton on these excursions, Uncle Joe used to say 'That's a Marston's place over there,' or 'That's a Strong's place.' He still remembered all the pubs. Once I was taking him to see one of his friends and he was giving me instructions as to which way to go. He kept peering through his thick-pebble glasses, 'I think its that turning on the right,' or 'No, its not, its a bit further on,' or, 'Perhaps we've passed it,' all the time shaking my arm in his excitement, and I was shouting back at him, 'Don't worry Uncle, we'll find it, it must be about here somewhere!' We came to a stretch of road which he immediately recognized and he bawled in my ear, 'Stop, stop, Nance! It's that turning on the right!' I stopped, put my hand out of the window to signal and waited to turn. Uncle enthusiastically jerked away at my arm – any moment now and he would be seeing Flossie. 'She can bang out any old tune that you like on the old Joanna,' he bellowed in my ear. 'We've had some jolly good sing-songs with old Flossie in the pub.'

The road junction quickly became a confusion of horn-blowing cars, and even a bus joined in. I wondered what all the noise was about. I looked out of my window, and the busdriver called down to me 'It's a no-right turn, missus – can't you read?' There was only one thing to do to get out of the mess, so I cheekily made a right-hand turn and disappeared down the no-entrance street. Fortunately, there wasn't a policeman about. Uncle Joe said that they had no right to put a one-way street there. We had a further minor excitement when I had stopped to get Uncle Joe some of his favourite 'Victory V' lozenges before taking him back to the Old People's home and I couldn't get the van to start. What was I to do? He didn't want to get back late as they were having his favourite dish, fish, for tea. There wasn't a telephone box in sight to ring for a taxi, and Uncle Joe certainly couldn't walk. With my usual rashness, and quite without thought, I left the van with Uncle in it, and placed myself in the middle of the road where, as if I were a traffic warden, I held up the first car that came along. A curly-haired young man was at the wheel. 'I've got a deaf, nearly-blind old man in my van, who cannot walk,' I said to him, 'Please could you give him a lift to Archers Road? It's not far from here and I'll pay you for it.' I explained to him that my van had broken down. He drove his car alongside my van and lifted Uncle out, as if it had just been all in a day's work. He wouldn't take any money, and he waved at me from his car window as he went off with Uncle Joe.

As Uncle Joe became older and weaker, I had to stop taking him out but still visited him until he died at the age of seventy-five. Sandra, too, had been a great comfort to him in his old age. Aunt Bell was a widow when she died in Hospital from old age; smiling, and making jokes and planning what she would do till the very end. She was eighty-two. Aunt Flo lasted the longest and died the year after Aunt Bell, aged eighty-four.

I went to have a look around Northam the other day. It only takes ten minutes by car to drive around the entire district. Most of it now is a small industrial estate, with a few blocks of modern, high-rise council flats by the river. The pavements are no longer gritty, for the Gas Works doesn't burn coal anymore and no longer belches forth the grey particle-laden filth. People now don't burn as much coal as they used to, so the coal yards are not as busy as they were. Everything seems to be smaller. The tiled front gardens where I played dibs with other children seemed hardly big enough to have contained the four or so of us, who squatted there as youngsters. The big wall against which I played as a girl has gone, and the tall gates which I climbed over as a teenager have been replaced. The lower end of Radcliffe Road is no more, and 'Bill Stickers' has vanished from the wall. Whatever lessons I learned from Northam were learned well, and I am rather like Mum in the way that I am always grateful that I can stand on my legs, and see out of my eyes. If anybody should ask me what I enjoy most of all, on reflection, I think I should answer 'Breathing'.

Nowadays, although I have lived in my present house for twenty years, I doubt if I could tell you the name of more than half-a-dozen people in our road. In the old Northam days, I knew all of our neighbours. Everybody is now so busy rushing off to work, including myself, that there is no time to 'Stand and stare'.

The doorbell rang the other day, and I opened it to find the splendidly erect figure of a woman in her mid-sixties. She was selling programmes for her local church bazaar. As I bought one from her, she said to me, 'I used to live in this house you know.' I was surprised at this, and it was her turn to be surprised when I asked, 'Don't you remember me, Miss Evans?' She vaguely remembered me she thought. 'I've had so many children pass through my hands over the years, it's a job to remember them all.' My thought was that 'No – but I will never forget you.' Such an excellent teacher, a credit to her profession, they don't seem to make them like her any more either. I wonder what she would think of today's discipline in our schools. Imagine trying to call her by *her* Christian name. She and her fellow teachers at Northam School taught large classes, but they were given the respect which was their due, and how they earned it!

When, over the years, I cycled to work, on odd occasions, I would pass a solid, balding middle-aged man on his bike, who would sort of nod at me, and I would sort of nod back, and he would then give me a wry grin. He was the youth who had trailed behind me pleading: 'You won't tell your brother will you?'